KT-590-534

HOW TO MANAGE YOUR STUDY TIME

Sharon Brophy

LEARNING SKILLS SERIES

HOW TO MANAGE YOUR STUDY TIME

Roger Lewis

NATIONAL
EXTENSION
COLLEGE

Collins Educational

© National Extension College Trust Ltd and Collins Educational 1994
This book is copyright under the Berne Convention.
No reproduction without permission. All rights reserved.

Published by Collins Educational
An imprint of Harper*Collins Publishers*
77–85 Fulham Palace Road
Hammersmith
London W6 8JB

First published in 1994

The National Extension College (NEC) is an educational trust with a distinguished body of trustees. Since it was established in 1963, it has pioneered the development of flexible learning for adults. NEC is actively developing innovative materials and systems for distance learning on over 100 courses, from basic skills to degree and professional training. Working in partnership with Collins Educational, NEC can now offer the best in flexible learning materials to the widest possible audience and further its aim of extending educational opportunities for all.

About the author:

Roger Lewis has taught in primary and secondary schools, adult and higher education. He is currently BP Professor of Learning Development at the University of Humberside. He has written many books for students and teachers.

The publishers wish to thank Tim Burton for his invaluable editorial expertise.

British Library Cataloguing-in-Publication Data
A catalogue record for
this book is
available from
the British Library

ISBN 0 00 322364 7

Typeset by Create Publishing Services Ltd, Bath.
Printed by HarperCollins Manufacturing, Glasgow.

Acknowledgements

The author would like to acknowledge the help given by the teachers and students who read and commented on the draft of this book, with thanks especially to Richard Baker; Bob Hunter, for help with the glossary; Lynn Inglis; Dina Lewis; Eunice Mathers, for help with the section on stress; Nigel Paine, for help with the section on electronic organisers; Rachel Sallis, for help with presentation of the manuscript; Roy Tunnicliffe.

The text was piloted in a number of institutions including Cambridge Regional College, the National Extension College, Leeds College of Technology and the University of Humberside. Acknowledgement is made to the help of Elaine Caicedo, Vivienne Eastwood, Anne Fallon, and Jim Nyland.

The author would also like to thank Tim Burton for his helpful comments and understanding throughout the writing process.

Contents

UNIT 1

INTRODUCING THIS BOOK

What this unit is about

Welcome to *How To Manage Your Study Time*. Most books about time management are written for people at work or in business. This book is different: it concentrates on the needs of the student in a wide range of educational situations. You may be studying in a further or higher education college, at school or in a sixth form college. You may be in an adult evening class or studying by open learning. You may be on a training course. Wherever and whatever you are studying, you will have to manage your own time. This book will help you with this. In particular it will help you complete your assignments effectively, by the due dates.

Managing time need not be difficult, but it does require thought and practice. Some books take a complicated approach, expecting you to buy expensive diary systems with accompanying stationery. This book makes the issues comprehensible, and uses resources you already have to hand.

This first unit will help you:

→ recognise the main features used in this book;

→ identify the approach the book takes to managing time;

→ decide where to start;

→ decide how you want to use the book.

The unit should take you approximately 1 hour to work through.

The book covers the key skills of managing time. You will find these listed on the Contents page, as unit headings. Each unit can be studied on its own, so you do not necessarily need to work through the book in strict order. But you should read this introductory unit carefully. It is also recommended that you work through Unit 2: understanding the demands of your course is an important, though not immediately obvious, aspect of managing your time. You will find more information on how to use the book in the section *Deciding where to start* on page 9.

Features

The book has been carefully constructed to be used as a tool. To get the maximum benefit from it you will need to do more than just read it through. A number of features have been included to stimulate the thought and action essential if you are to use your time more productively.

■ Unit introductions outlining what the unit should help you do, together with guidance on the time you should expect to spend and any resources you will need.

- A discussion of the key skill covered in the unit. The advice is based on generally agreed good practice. You do need, though, to test this out thoroughly, to see if it works for you.

- Examples to show how the skill can be put into practice. These are usually kept simple, free of unnecessary detail, to isolate key points. It's not possible to use examples from every reader's course, so you'll need to think about the general principles underlying the examples. Try to relate them to the subjects you are studying.

- Activities, providing opportunities for you to think about the skills, with immediate feedback on each. You should write down your responses to the activities before reading on. Use a sheet of file paper for this, so you can build up a record of your progress and decisions. Cover up the responses if you feel you may be tempted to read on before you have prepared your own response.

- Comments made by other students on how they have tackled a particular time management issue.

- Projects to give you the chance to try things out and experiment with new ways of managing your time. Through the projects you can adapt the advice to the way you work best – to your temperament and to the course you are taking. As with activities, use file paper to record the results of your projects.

- Checklists, summary lists of key points or questions. These help you in a number of ways, for example to carry out a task or to draw up an action plan.

- Action plans to help you set manageable targets for improvement. Use file paper or a diary, whichever is appropriate, for your planning work.

- A glossary and further reading section. You will find these two sections at the end of the book. The glossary defines key words. These are emphasised by bold type when you first meet them in the main text. The further reading list guides you to sources of more detailed help or information on particular topics.

The approach taken by the book

The approach taken can be summarised as follows.

- Changing the way you manage your time means changing your behaviour.

- We can all change our behaviour.

- We do not change just by reading or talking about it: we have to be active.

- Changing behaviour takes time. It needs practice and reflection.

So the good news is that you can improve the way you manage time. But you have to make an effort to do it. The first activity gives you a chance to see what's involved.

Think of an attempt you have recently made to change your behaviour. If you find this difficult, think of a friend or relative who has made the effort. Examples could be:

- to lose weight;
- to get fit;
- to be more friendly to a particular person;

(continued opposite)

- to stop smoking;
- to get up earlier in the mornings.

First, how far did you succeed in your attempt?

Second, write down the reasons why you (or the friend) succeeded (or failed!).

As with all the activities, you should write down your responses first. Don't read on until you have done this. Students sometimes find it helpful to cover up the next section until they have completed their own answers.

Here are some reasons why we do succeed in changing our behaviour.

- We really want to change.

- We set ourselves a clear end goal – for example to jog three times each week, for a minimum of 30 minutes each time.

- We set targets en route to the goal. These are detailed and specific, making it possible to measure success. For example, start by jogging twice each week for 10 minutes each time, gradually increasing this.

- We get other people to help – for example asking a friend to jog with us.

- We keep practising the new skill until it becomes second nature.

- We think about the techniques we are using, adjusting them when necessary.

The reasons for failure tend to be the reverse of these.

This book will help you take all the necessary positive steps set out above. It will support you as you try out new ways of managing your time. You will be encouraged to aim not at perfection – none of us can achieve that – but at making significant improvements. Sometimes small steps will make a recognisable difference. Each unit will ask you to review where you currently are on each aspect of time management, and to identify the specific steps you want to take.

Deciding where to start

You can work systematically through the book from start to finish, if you wish. Or you may choose to skim through the book, returning later to units of special interest. A further option is to identify an area of time management that particularly concerns you. In this case, the questions below will help. Tick the box that best applies to you in each case (try to be honest with yourself!). You can answer the questions even if you are returning to study after a long break. Then read the notes that follow.

1   When starting a new **course**, do you find out as much as you can about it, and in particular how, when and how often you will be assessed?

Usually ☐   Sometimes ☐   Never ☐

2   Many students have to prepare several different pieces of work all at the same time. In this book these are called **assignments**. Faced with this challenge, do you plan in advance when you will work on the various stages of each assignment?

Usually ☐   Sometimes ☐   Never ☐

3   Before you begin a particular assignment, do you work out exactly what is expected of you?

Usually ☐   Sometimes ☐   Never ☐

4   Do you start assignments when you feel like it, without worrying too much about whether you have all the necessary resources to hand?

Usually ☐   Sometimes ☐   Never ☐

5   Do you break large tasks into smaller ones and work out how long each will take?

Usually ☐   Sometimes ☐   Never ☐

6   Can you work out approximately how much time next week you will have available for your own private study – that is, after necessary activities like eating, sleeping and attending classes?

Usually ☐   Sometimes ☐   Never ☐

7   Do you regularly draw up a plan for how you will use your time the next day?

Usually ☐   Sometimes ☐   Never ☐

8   Do you often delay work, putting it off until later?

Usually ☐   Sometimes ☐   Never ☐

9   Do you allow yourself to be interrupted while working?

Usually ☐   Sometimes ☐   Never ☐

10   Do you often lose or mislay the papers, files, notes, etc. that you need for your study?

Usually ☐   Sometimes ☐   Never ☐

11   Do you get annoyed because your workspace (desk, etc.) is disorganised, making it difficult to get down to work?

Usually ☐   Sometimes ☐   Never ☐

12   Do you feel under stress because you don't seem to have enough time to do all that is expected of you?

Usually ☐   Sometimes ☐   Never ☐

13   Do you use other people to help you manage your time?

Usually ☐   Sometimes ☐   Never ☐

14   Do you use a diary or other time management system to help you manage your time?

Usually ☐   Sometimes ☐   Never ☐

15   Do you regularly review how effectively you have used your time?

Usually ☐   Sometimes ☐   Never ☐

As you will have guessed, in each case one answer is 'right' in that it shows what is usually considered good time management practice. In reality, none of us is perfect, that's why USUALLY is the heading rather than ALWAYS! If you ticked SOMETIMES quite a lot this may show that you are organised when you make a special effort. Read the responses for each individual question. The general comments at the end will help you interpret your results.

1   The best answer is USUALLY. To get an overview of your course helps you plan your use of time. The assessment requirements are particularly important, since these will be used to determine your success on the course. If you ticked NEVER this might be a priority area for you. It is covered in Unit 2.

2   The best answer is USUALLY. Students often have to tackle a number of assignments at once, for example for different **modules** of their course. It is good practice to plan exactly when you will work on the different stages of each assignment. If you answered NEVER, Unit 3 might help you with this important aspect of managing your time.

3   The best answer is USUALLY. If you know exactly what your tutor expects, you can use the time you have available to produce an assignment that meets the necessary criteria. If you ticked NEVER you might choose to work through Unit 4.

4   This time the best answer is NEVER. You generally save time in the long run if you first collect all the necessary resources for an assignment. If you ticked USUALLY you might start with Unit 5.

5   USUALLY is the best answer. Breaking tasks into small activities helps you move steadily toward your goal. This is covered in Unit 6.

6   Ideally you will have ticked USUALLY. A person who appreciates the value of time knows what they have available over the forthcoming week. If you ticked NEVER, try Unit 7.

7   The best answer is USUALLY. Drawing up (and following!) a time plan for the next day helps you achieve your objectives. If you don't usually do this, Unit 7 will help.

8   If you NEVER put work off you are doing well already! If you USUALLY delay work, make Unit 8 an early priority.

9   Ideally, you have ticked NEVER. By definition, interruptions stop us doing what we want to do. Most of us, however, are less than perfect and would probably tick SOMETIMES. But if you ticked USUALLY you may have a problem here, and so choose to tackle Unit 9.

10   If you ticked NEVER then you already keep your papers under perfect control – a sign of good time management. If you USUALLY lose things you might turn to Unit 10.

11   If your workspace is in a constant muddle and this hinders you, you will have ticked USUALLY. If you ticked NEVER then you already practise the time management skill of controlling your workspace. You may have been surprised to see this topic raised, but organising your work environment contributes to time efficiency. If you want to work further at this, see Unit 10.

12   If you are right on top of your work, and can complete everything well in time, you will have ticked NEVER. If you USUALLY feel stressed this might be a priority area for you, in which case Unit 11 should help. It's very difficult to change your behaviour when you are seriously stressed, so even if you ticked SOMETIMES you should still consider tackling Unit 11.

13   It's good practice to identify people who can help you use your time well, so USUALLY is a good answer. Unit 12 should help you if you haven't thought of this aspect of good time managment.

14 Diaries or other systems can be useful for controlling time. Unit 12 will help you consider how you might benefit from them.

15 USUALLY is the best answer. It is good practice to stand back and analyse how effectively you have used your time. Indeed, conscious review helps you improve any learning skill. If you NEVER review your use of time, look at Unit 13.

Please note the points that follow.

The above answers are only guides. It is possible, for example, to work productively surrounded by muddled papers; never to draw up a written daily plan but still to spend the day purposefully. Possible, but unlikely. The 'right' answers are right in the sense that they are generally considered good practice, the experience of most people. You may, of course, be the exception that proves the rule. But think hard about it first.

You may well have ticked SOMETIMES quite often. In this case you have to decide which are the priority areas for you. The action plan below should help you do this.

Your use of this book

You can begin your time management by thinking about how and when you will use this book. One important skill is to timetable tasks to the most suitable times. For example, plan to tackle difficult tasks when you are fresh and unlikely to be disturbed. You also need to give yourself a variety of challenges, so you are less likely to grow bored.

Will you be able to use others to help you develop your time management skills? Working with one or two other students can help you stay keen and make progress. Unit 12 returns to this.

2

Ask yourself the following questions:

■ When do you do your best work – early in the morning; at night?

■ Where do you like to work – in the library, at home?

■ When are you usually able to work undisturbed?

■ Will you work with other people? If so, who?

We all have different preferences. One of the aims of this book is to help you recognise your own best study routines and to build on these. Your responses to the activity will help you put together your action plan.

When and where will you study this book? Will you study with others? Jot down, on your file paper, times in the day, places and people.

Which parts of the book will you study? Use the box below to select your first three priorities. (Leave your choice of subsequent topics until later.)

Priority	Unit

Conclusion

Good luck with your work on time management. You should enjoy some of the following benefits:

- ■ you work smarter (not necessarily harder);

- ■ you create time for other things in your life as well as study;

- ■ you are efficient when you need to be (not necessarily all the time!)

To encourage you on your journey, here are the comments of some other students.

> I can find things more easily. I don't have to make so many excuses for things that I've forgotten or that are late.

> I feel more confident, and cope better with other people's demands on my time.

> I've a clearer view of what I really do have to do, and what will wait.

> I plan ahead better. I don't feel things are hanging over me. I used to overplan and at times it became a substitute for action. But now I know when to plan and in how much detail.

UNIT 2

ASSESSING THE DEMANDS OF DIFFERENT COURSES

What this unit is about

This unit will help you:

→ identify the learning **objectives** of your course (the **outcomes**);

→ anticipate how you will be assessed;

→ outline the way your **course** is structured.

Time: approximately 30 minutes. You will need at least a further 30 minutes for the project, assuming all the necessary information is to hand.

Resources: file paper, for notes; information on your course, particularly on its learning outcomes, content and structure.

The key skill dealt with in this unit is how to assess the overall demands made by your course. This will help you plan your work, and in particular how to use your time. You will also be able to use the information for other units in this book.

You should note that different institutions use different terms to describe the way courses are put together. 'Unit', 'module', 'programme' and 'course' can thus mean different things. The glossary defines the way the terms are used in this book. But you need to find out what they mean in your own school, college or university.

Different courses make different demands on your planning skills.

Some examples are shown below.

Course	Planning requirement
A business studies course with continuous assessment and a work placement, leading to a project.	Assignments must be in on time. You have to fix the placement well in advance. While on placement, you need to anticipate, and collect, information for the project.
Traditional 'A' level course. Final exams decide your grade.	You have to maintain your impetus over a long period. You have to plan your revision carefully, as so much depends on the exam.

Course	Planning requirement
A National Vocational Qualification to be gained while in employment.	You need to draw up an action plan with your manager and an assessor. You have to agree arrangements to visit other sections in the workplace. You have to collect evidence and organise it, to demonstrate your competence in carrying out tasks.

These are three differently structured courses. Each makes distinctive demands on the student. Your first job is thus to find out, as exactly as possible and in advance, what your course expects of you. This important information can be set out under three headings: the course's learning outcomes (what you are expected to learn); the assessment regulations (how your learning will be measured); and the way the course is structured (including the timetable).

> Once I got a picture of the whole course I could see how the various bits fitted together.

Learning outcomes

Increasingly, courses set out the outcomes you, the student, are expected to achieve. **National Vocational Qualifications (NVQs)** and **General National Vocational Qualification (GNVQs)** organise the outcomes into 'units', 'elements' and 'performance criteria'. The following example is from the draft specification for GNVQ Sciences, Level 3.

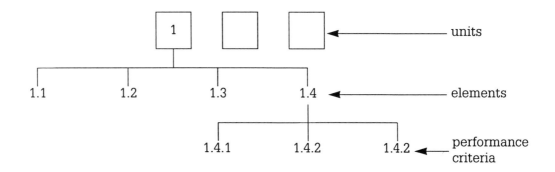

Source: RSA Examinations board

There is not space here to define 'unit', 'element' or 'performance criteria', or the additional ingredients of standards, such as 'range' and 'evidence indicator'. Nor can we show the GNVQ programme in its entirety. If you were studying such a programme you would have to find all these things out, asking tutors as necessary.

You should, however, be able to see from the above example how such a programme is organised. The elements and performance criteria set out the learning outcomes: what you have to be able to do to demonstrate your **competence**. Element 1.4, for example, is 'Evaluate data from secondary sources'. The three performance criteria for this are:

1.4.1   Secondary sources are identified

1.4.2   More than one source is used to check reliability

1.4.3   Relevance of data and information is determined

Other programmes are differently set out. GCSE English, for example, lists 'assessment objectives' under the headings of Speaking and Listening, Reading and Writing. A typical objective is 'communicate a sensitive and informed personal response to what is heard, read or seen'.

The value of learning outcomes is that you can spot in advance the kind of work you have to produce to succeed. Admittedly the language can be dry and complex. But you can ask your tutor for help. You soon get used to it!

Unfortunately some courses don't state any outcomes. If you're lucky you may be handed a 'syllabus' – a list of topics or subjects, with little or no indication of what you are supposed to do as a result of studying them. Here is an example.

CONTENT

1.   What is Europe? – Europe East and West, the Common European Home, the European Economic space. The collapse of communism in the East, and the emergent liberal democracies. A redefining of the roles of the Warsaw Pact and NATO. The impact of reduced military spending. Privatising and restructuring Eastern European industry.

2.   Integration Theory – Interdependency theories, functionalism, neo-functionalism, transactionalism, federalism, intergovernmentalism. Theory of customs unions, political and economic integration.

Source: NEC GCSE English

This gives you useful information on the content you will cover. But you need to find out what it means in terms of the work you have to produce. Tutors, past students and examination papers can all help you with this.

> I was in the dark before. I didn't know what they wanted. Once I saw outcomes on paper, I could see what I was working towards.

Assessment requirements

You also need to know how you will be assessed. How will your tutor(s) and examiner(s) decide whether or not you have succeeded in achieving the learning outcomes? If you are preparing for a G/NVQ you will have to decide what kinds of evidence of your competence you will collect.

Sometimes assessment information is helpfully summarised in a booklet, given out at the start of your course. The example below is from GCSE English. If your course has such a booklet, you should refer to it frequently, to remind yourself of key points.

Exam and Coursework Guide

If you are planning to take the GCSE exam, you should read this guide carefully. It contains important information about the exam and the coursework assignments. Coursework counts for 20% of your final exam mark. The guide also contains some specimen questions to help you to practise for the written exam.

Source: NEC GCSE English

Assessment these days is much more varied than in the past. More use is made of realistic contexts, such as the workplace. More information on what tutors are looking for in your work is usually available. All this has implications for your time planning. Generally, you need to be better organised, for example in collecting examples of your work in a **portfolio**. Planning for each individual assessment activity is covered in Unit 4.

The checklist summarises what you need to know about assessment.

Checklist

Do I know:

● what form the assessment will take – for example essays, group projects?

● any general assessment regulations – for example about assignment length?

● whether assessment is continuous – that is, does work set during the course count towards the final result?

● whether assessment takes place only at the end of the course, as in a final exam?

● assignment titles and dates?

Course structure

You need to see how your course is put together. The example below is for a student on a degree course.

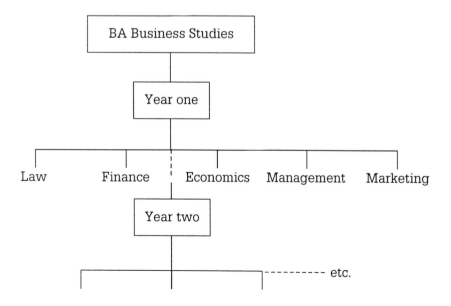

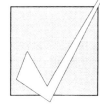

Checklist

The following checklist will help you identify what you need to know about the structure of your course.

Do I have the following information about my course:

● its title;

● its length;

● its component parts;

● what is compulsory;

● what is optional?

You then need to move down a level to find out how each component part of your course (such as each **module**) is structured.

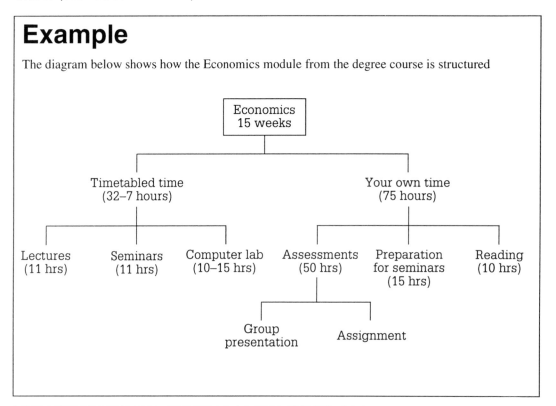

Example

The diagram below shows how the Economics module from the degree course is structured

Checklist

For each component, do I know:

● its length;

● time spent in lectures and seminars, etc.;

● time spent in labs, workshops, on field work, etc.;

● time spent in self-directed study?

As with assessment information, you will sometimes be given all the relevant information. The following extract is from a study guide for GCSE English.

How long will the course take?

Each unit is self-contained and designed to take you about 1–2 hours of study-time. You can work through the units at your own speed, as fast or as slowly as you like but if you study every unit the course will take you about 100 hours. (You should allow more time than this if you intend to do a lot of extra reading.) Most learners take around 9 months to complete the course, but it is up to you to learn in your own way.

Source: NEC GCSE English

Unfortunately, the world is an imperfect place. You cannot always rely on clarity. Some of the information you need may not be written down. Students are assumed somehow to know it, without being told! Tutors sometimes set assignments without giving you enough notice, or any information about the time the assignment might take. You will have to persist in getting the information you need. It is vital to your planning. Unit 12 suggests who you might turn to for help.

> **Even if you do try to manage your time the lecturers mess it up for you. They spring things on you. I wish the lecturers would manage their time; that would help us manage ours.**

The project for this unit is to find out as much as possible about your own course. In particular:

- its learning outcomes – what you are expected to do;

- its assessment requirements – how your performance will be assessed;

- its structure, and in particular how your time will be spent.

If possible, draw a diagram to show this structure. Use the earlier checklists as a guide.

Action plan

You may well have found some gaps in the information you collected. The action plan will help you to complete the picture. Draw a table like the one below and list:

- the information/resources you still need;

- how you will collect this;

- who will help you;

- when you will start and finish.

The final column is for comment on your progress.

Information/ resources	How collected	Who will help	Dates	Comment

UNIT 3

PLANNING SEVERAL ASSIGNMENTS

What this unit is about

This unit will help you:

→ identify **assignments** that have to be carried out in parallel;

→ schedule the tasks you need to carry out, to complete these assignments by the due dates.

Time: approximately 20 minutes to work through the unit, with an additional 40 minutes for the project.

Resources: file paper; titles of assignments you have to complete; a time period in which you have to complete the assignments.

As a student you'll often have to complete several assignments within a particular time period, such as a **term**. These assignments may vary widely, including, for example, an experiment, a group presentation, a report and an essay. Each of these requires a different approach, with a wide range of activities to be planned along the way. So being able to plan to complete several assignments, all of which have to be handed in at around the same time, is a crucial skill.

Units 4, 5 and 6 give more detail on how to tackle an individual assignment, including a detailed breakdown of the tasks you have to complete and how to schedule them. This unit looks more generally at how you plan several parallel assignments.

1 What are the consequences of poor planning? Can you think of a specific case when you failed to plan well? What happened?

Here are some familiar results.

I missed the deadlines.

> I got the assignment in but only with last-minute stress.

> When I settled down to work I found I hadn't got the resources I needed.

> I concentrated on one project and did well on that. But I got poor marks on the others.

This unit describes an approach you can use to avoid these pitfalls. If you follow this approach you will:

- meet deadlines;

- feel comfortably in control throughout;

- have all the necessary resources to hand, at the right time;

- perform consistently on all your assignments.

The four stages of planning

The suggested stages are set out briefly below, with examples. You are then invited to try the approach out for yourself.

1. Write down the assignments and the time period in which you have to complete them.

Example

Three assignments to complete in the autumn term:

- a 'business game' (for economics);

- a marketing assignment requiring an interview with the local supermarket manager;

- a law assignment involving access to on-line **databases**.

2. For each assignment, list the main tasks you have to complete. Put these into the right order.

Example

For the marketing assignment I knew I would have to:

- interview supermarket manager;

- read and make notes;

- write the report.

3. Draw up a timetable. On this insert the end dates for the completion of each assignment. Then add the tasks you listed at 2 above, with dates (see the example below).

4. Add your other major commitments during the relevant time period (see the left hand column in the example below). Make any necessary adjustments, for example to avoid bottlenecks.

Example

The student has summarised the assignments at the top and then listed the main tasks for each, with dates and approximate times.

Other Commitments	Economics: business game set 8 Oct; due 11 Nov			Marketing set 3 Oct; due 9 Nov			Law set 1 Nov; due 8 Nov		
	Date	Activity	Duration	Date	Activity	Duration	Date	Activity	Duration
Football every Wed pm (2 hrs) 10–12 Oct: visit Tasha in Oxford	8 Oct	1st meeting	2 hours	6 Oct; 14–17 Nov	Identify research; read; make notes	20 hours			
	15 Oct	2nd meeting	2 hours						
	22 Oct	3rd meeting	2 hours						
	28 Oct	Final meeting	2 hours	29 Oct–1 Nov	Write report	8 hours			
30–31 Oct go to Pat's wedding in Scotland	2–11 Nov	Prepare report and presentation	15 hours	4–9 Nov	Type report	8 hours	1 Nov	Book database session; identify information sources	4 hours

Project

Now schedule the assignments from your own course, using the approach described in this unit. Work through the four stages described earlier, applying them to your own situation.

Conclusion

You may need to practise this several times, until the process becomes second nature. Once you have a general plan for, say, a term or a year you can plan each individual assignment in more detail. This is dealt with in the next three units.

> Once I'd set out all my assignments I could relax. I could see how I could fit them all in. I knew when I could take my breaks, as well.

UNIT 4 DEFINING THE TASK

What this unit is about

This unit will help you:

→   identify the outcome expected from an assignment;

→   list the characteristics of a successful assignment.

Time: approximately 30 minutes to work through the unit; a further 30 minutes for the project.

Resources: file paper, an assignment you have to tackle.

Unit 2 pointed out the importance of finding out as much as possible about the assessment requirements of your course. This unit turns to the level of the individual assignment: what should it look like and what criteria will your tutor use to assess it?

Assignment outcomes

First, how much guidance are you given on what your work should look like? Some programmes provide plenty of clear information on this, others give little or no direction. Three familiar situations are described below.

1.   You are given a very explicit statement of outcomes.

Example

Your portfolio should contain at least five letters and five internal memoranda. The letters should be a minimum of 150 words each, with each letter including at least two paragraphs. They should be word processed.

Extract from assignment information
for a course on business administration

2.   You are given some information on the end product, for example indicating the length and presentation requirements.

Example

Write between 300 and 400 words, including at least three paragraphs. Your answer can be handwritten, typed or word processed. Please leave generous margins around your work.

Extract from assignment information
for an English course

3. You are given only very sketchy information on what your answer should look like.

Example

Write a report on the availability of low-alchohol drinks in your neighbourhood

Extract from assignment information
for a marketing programme

1 What additional information would you need if you were answering the assignment in Example 3?

It would be helpful to know:

■ the required length of the report;

■ sections to be included, such as an introduction and recommendations.

2 Assume you are set an assignment with little information on the expected outcome. What action should you take?

You should find out as much as possible, preferably from the person who is assessing the report. Otherwise you risk wasting time and getting a poor mark simply because you misunderstood what was expected. Time spent clarifying the outcome can save a lot of time later. If you are in any doubt you should add a note with your assignment, explaining why you have tackled the assignment in a particular way, as in the example below.

Example

I have included the survey detail but as an appendix. I have assumed this will not count in the overall word length for the assignment.

Criteria for a successful assignment

Here we turn to the qualities of a successful assignment: the **criteria** your tutor will use to assess your work. The range of possibilities is similar to those discussed in the previous section on outcomes.

1. You may be given a detailed list of criteria, together with the marks you will gain for each. You may need to ask for help in interpreting these.

Read the extract below, which comes from a business studies course. Write down one or two questions you would ask your tutor to help you understand the criteria.

**Indicative Assessment Scheme: Assignment 1
(Group project)**

Assessment area and criteria		Percentage mark for area
1 Justification for project management technique		20%
i	explanation of general reasons for failure of original project *range–detailed/very delivery/none*	5%
ii	identification of specific areas that led to failure of original project *range–detailed/very general/none*	5%
iii	explanation of advantages project management approach would have offered *range–fully justified/general/poorly justified*	10%

You might ask the following questions:

■ What does 'indicative' mean?

■ What does 'range' mean?

2. You may get some information to guide you, but still be left with questions.

Read the following example. Then write down some questions you would want to ask before you tackled it.

The main purpose of this assignment is to encourage you to write something your tutor can use as a basis for drawing up a study plan with you. Write about the past 24 hours. Pick out particularly interesting things that happened, people you met or places you visited. Do not try to cover everything that happened.

You might ask questions such as the following:

■ How important is grammar?

■ Will marks be lost for poor punctuation and spelling?

You might also ask questions relating to some aspect of the outcome, such as length and presentation, for example.

3. You may be given no information at all on the characteristics of a successful assignment.

Look back at the earlier example of the report on low-alcohol drinks. Again, what questions might you ask?

There are many possibilities here, including:

■ Who is the report for?

■ Is a particular survey method to be used?

■ Is evidence of additional reading required?

Case study 1: Outcomes and criteria

This section works through a fairly typical example. It shows Jean, a student, identifying the information needed on both the outcome and characteristics of an assignment. It also shows how she finds this out. You can then use a similar strategy in your project for this unit.

Jean is set the following assignment.

Join with three other students in your seminar group. Carry out a survey of the use of **CD-ROM** in your site library. How could this usage be increased? Hand in a report. Your group will make a presentation, based on the report, to the other members of the seminar.

What further information would Jean need? **Brainstorm** the questions you might ask the tutor who set the assignment. Consider both outcomes and assessment criteria.

You might start with the kinds of question suggested earlier in this unit. You might, for example, ask how long the report should be and for how many minutes the presentation is expected to last. Who is the report intended for? As always, you should find out as much as possible about assessment, especially as, in this case, group assessment is involved. Some questions here might be:

■ How will marks be distributed for the report?

■ How will the presentation be assessed?

■ Do we all get the same grade or are we assessed as individuals?

To ask questions like these is the sign of a good student. The second step is to uncover the answers. Here you may have to act rather like a detective. You won't always get answers to all your questions. Sometimes the tutor will expect you to use your initiative – and that's fine, as long as you know this in advance.

In our example Jean took her questions to the tutor. She found out a lot of useful information, including the following.

Example

Length

Flexible, but six A4 sides would probably be about right for the report (250 words maximum per side).

Maximum 15 minutes for the presentation, with an additional 10 minutes for questions and discussion.

Audience

Assume you are advising the senior site librarian, who wishes to promote the CD-ROM resource more widely within the institution.

Allocation of marks for the report

Evidence of reading and research: 10.

Clarity of language (style, grammar, spelling, punctuation, etc.): 10.

Good final presentation (word processed, etc.): 10.

Practicality of the recommendations: 10.

Discussion of cost implications: 10.

Allocation of marks for the presentation

A clear structure: 10.

Interesting and attractive vocal delivery (tone, variety, etc.): 10.

Good non-verbal behaviour (posture, eye contact, dress, etc.): 10.

Good use of visual aids (e.g. overhead acetates): 10.

Ability to involve the audience and answer questions: (10).

Group assessment

The report will be assessed by the tutor and your group will be given one grade, i.e. the same grade for all members, regardless of individual contributions.

The presentation will be assessed by the audience of other students; again, one grade will be given.

This assessment is designed to encourage students to work responsibly together as a team.

Note in particular the useful detail contained in the brackets. This translates general points (such as 'good non-verbal behaviour') into specifics ('posture, eye contact and dress'). It took the student only 30 minutes to find all this out – a very productive use of time.

Ideally, you should ask your tutor for any additional information you need. Sometimes the tutor is not available – or even, maybe, unhelpful. In this case, where else could you turn for the information?

Here are some possibilities you might have noted:

- other tutors in the same department;
- staff in the library or resource centre;
- your fellow students, by putting your heads together to work out likely answers;
- students who have previously answered a similar assignment;
- previous assignments, which may be kept in the library;
- past exam papers.

Project

Choose an assignment from your course on which you will soon be working. Find out as much as you can about:

- what the end product should look like;
- the criteria the tutor will be using in assessing your work and how marks will be distributed.

Action plan

This action plan will help you prepare for future assignments. Answer the following questions, using a table like the one below.

- What assignments do you have to complete over the next period (term, year, etc.)?
- What questions should you ask about each?
- Who do you need to ask?
- When?

At the end, review how effective you were in your attempt to find the answers. Did you find out what you wanted to know? Could you have done so more easily?

Assignment title	Questions to ask	Who to ask	Date	Review

At the start it seemed to take a lot of time, working out what was required. But I found it made the assignment much easier to do. Thinking about it was part of doing it, I suppose.

UNIT 5 PLANNING TO SUCCEED IN THE TASK

What this unit is about

This unit will help you:

→ list the resources you will need for each assignment;

→ work out when you will need them, and for how long;

→ decide how you will get them;

→ draw up a resource plan.

Time: 30 minutes, and a further 60 minutes on the project.

Resources: file paper; an assignment on which you have to work.

First, a question: have you ever had this experience? You sit down to work on an assignment. At last you really think you can get into it. Within a few minutes, however, you find you haven't got certain important books or papers. You come to a stop.

Most of us have been in this situation all too often. It can be very frustrating to clear time for study, only to find the time is wasted. The problem is created by a lack of planning. The term 'plan' puts some people off. It sounds cold and rigid. In fact a plan should be the reverse. It is a flexible guide to doing things better.

This unit helps you plan the resources you will need for a forthcoming assignment, so you can then collect them well in advance. The project will give you practice. To complete it you will need an assignment title, preferably one which you know you have to complete in a few months' time. Ideally you will have teased out the requirements for this assignment, as described in Unit 4. You will thus know:

■ the title of the assignment and the date for handing it in;

■ what the assignment should look like;

■ criteria for success and, if possible, how marks will be awarded;

■ any stages you are recommended to use in completing the task.

You will use this assignment throughout the unit as the basis for identifying the resources you will need and how you will collect them. You will then need to practise on several other assignments, to get used to the stages.

Stage 1: What resources are needed?

The first stage is to work out what kinds of resource you need to complete the assignments set on your course.

1 Brainstorm the various resources you need on your course. Think of as many relevant resources as possible. If you wish, set these out in patterned form, as shown below.

Your response will depend on the nature of your course. Resources can be very varied, including those set out below.

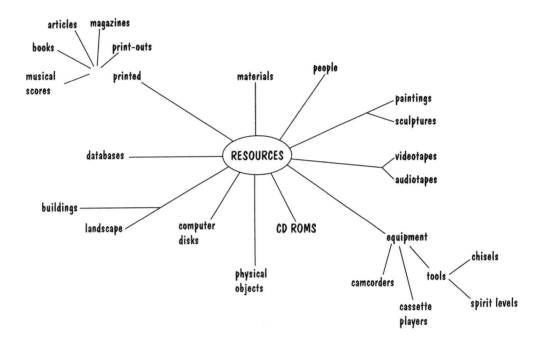

Physical resources are more important in some subjects than others. Engineering, brick-laying, architecture and geology, for example, all in their own ways make use of tools, equipment and the landscape. The social sciences make intensive use of people, for example through surveys and interviews.

You have looked generally at the resources you need for your course. You can now explore those you will need to answer the particular assignment you have chosen for this unit.

Project

Turn to your assignment. What resources will you need if you are to complete it successfully?

Think of the widest possible range of resources. It might be worth talking to a librarian: they are trained in the identification and use of resources of all kinds.

Example

An assignment for a marketing programme reads as follows:

Find out how many types of low-alcohol drinks are on sale in your local supermarket. Choose one brand and write a report for the supermarket manager on alternative ways of marketing this product. In your report you should consider such issues as:

- ■ direct and indirect costs;

- ■ promotional literature;

- ■ head office regulations on the conduct of promotional campaigns.

Your report should refer to current theory and practice in marketing, drawing on the resources to which you have been introduced earlier in your programme.

The student faced with this assignment would need to find out more, in the ways described in Unit 4. But there is sufficient information here to identify the resources a student would need. These would include:

- ■ the manager of at least one local supermarket, on two occasions – once for an interview at the start of the project, then later to comment on a draft of the report;

- ■ three business databases;

- ■ textbooks;

- ■ journals;

- ■ newspapers.

Stage 2:
When will you need these resources?

You now need to identify roughly when you will need the resources. To do this return to your rough plan of when you will be working on the various stages of the assignment. Unit 3 covered this.

Project

Take the assignment you have been working on in this unit. Draw up a rough plan that includes:

- ■ the main stages you will need to work through to complete the assignment;

- ■ when you plan to complete these stages;

- ■ how long (approximately) you expect each stage to take.

Note that you need list only the main stages (as in the examples in Unit 3): detailed planning for an assignment is covered in Unit 6.

Example

You'll see from Unit 3 that the marketing student plans to complete the assignment between 3 October and 9 November. But more detail is needed on exactly when the various resources will be needed. Hence the next stage.

Stage 3: Analysing the availability of the resources

You know the resources you have to get. But will they be available at the right time? You can't just assume you will get hold of the resources immediately.

Turn back to the list of resources you made in response to the first activity in this unit. These are the resources you might generally need for your course. For each type of resource ask yourself the questions set out in the checklist below.

Checklist

- Do I need to buy this or can I borrow/share it?

- Can I afford it?

- Is this generally available immediately or do I need to book it?

- For how long can I use this? What are the limits (for example, short-loan periods)?

- Will I be able to take this resource away to study it or do I have to use it in a fixed location?

- Do I know how to operate it?

- Will I need special equipment to use this resource?

It's difficult to predict your answers. Much will depend on your particular course. Here are some general comments.

> Booking: you may need to book access to databases in advance (this depends on the library). Inter-library loans also need to be pre-booked. You need appointments to gain access to some people – for example, employers, your tutor.

> Limited access time: times for book borrowing are usually limited; some resources are on very short term loan.

> Place: some resources are not allowed out of a library, archive or laboratory. Some resources are permanently fixed, for example the landscape and buildings. If you need experience in different jobs you obviously have to travel to particular locations for this, as in work placements.

> Equipment: you need equipment to use resources such as audio- and videotapes and computer software.

All this should show the need for careful planning and scheduling.

Project

Look at each resource you need for the particular assignment on which you have been working during this unit. Complete a table such as the following to show:

- which resources will have to be booked in advance (add details, such as the amount of notice you will need to give);

- any limits on the time you are allowed to use each resource;

- other limitations, such as the need to visit a particular location or use special equipment.

Resource	Notice	Duration limited to	Other limitations

Example

The example shows a selection from the marketing student's notes.

Resource	Notice	Duration limited to	Other limitations
Database	2 days	30 mins	Library
Interviews	2 weeks	2 sessions, each 1 hour	Supermarket
Inter-library loans	2–3 weeks	Books: 2 weeks only	–
Short-term loans	–	1 hour only	In library

Stage 4:
Drawing up your resource plan

You should now have all the information you need to plan:

■ when you will need the resources;

■ when you will have to book them;

■ length of time you can borrow/use each resource;

■ any special arrangements you have to make.

But you need to think about one other thing first: is it likely that other students will be wanting to use exactly the same resources as you, at exactly the same time? Student numbers are increasing rapidly; library and other resources are not growing at the same rate. So, again, you have to think ahead. You should schedule your use of scarce resources to times when you think it unlikely that other students will need them. This could mean working well in advance of the deadlines for handing in the assignment. Or working in the library in quiet times, such as evenings or weekends.

Example

The marketing student plans to start work on the assignment on 3 October. But a little forethought shows that some things need to be planned before then, particularly the interview with the supermarket manager. Here is an extract from the student's resource planning, taken from her file.

> 6/9: letter to s'mkt manager: what I am doing and how he can help. Suggest dates – one around 17/10, after prelim research; 2nd around 31/10 when report is in draft. Say I'll phone to confirm.
>
> 13/9: phone manager to book the two appointments.

This careful planning should mean that the student will have the resources available at the right times. Here is an extract from her detailed timetable. Note that this includes dates, actions, how long each action should take.

> 16/10: prepare for meeting with supermarket manager. Draw up in advance a list of questions to ask (1 hour 30 mins).
>
> 17/10: interview supermarket manager (1 hour interview; 1 hour travel).
>
> 18/10: write up notes of interview (1 hour 30 mins).
>
> (18/10 – 25/10: work on other assignments).
>
> 26/10 – 28/10: items booked on 5/10 should be available now. Read these and make notes. NB resources have to be returned by 2/11 (4 hours).
>
> 28/10 – 1/11: first draft of the report (4 hours).
>
> 2/11: present report to supermarket manager (1 hour; 1 hour travel).

Project

Draw up a detailed timetable to ensure that:

- you book the resources in advance;
- you timetable in your diary or planner when you will use the resources;
- you include the study time you expect to need.

Conclusion

The planning described in this unit has the following three advantages.

> It forces you to think in detail about what you have to do.
>
> It means you can use your time positively when you do sit down to work on the assignment.
>
> It can reveal setbacks, which you can raise in advance with your tutor.

But you do need to work through the stages for several assignments, to get fully used to this method of detailed advanced planning.

Action plan

Tackle this when you have had several opportunities to practise the method recommended in this unit. (Put a date in your diary to do this.)

What improvements do you need to make to the ways in which you plan and collect resources? The checklist below summarises the advice given in this unit.

Checklist

Do I:

- analyse each assignment to decide what resources are necessary?
- consider a wide range of types of resource?
- plan when resources will be needed?
- plan for how long they will be needed?
- identify those that will have to be booked in advance?
- identify those that may be available for only a limited period of time?
- identify those that will have to be consulted in a special place?
- identify those that will need special equipment?
- plan to use resources when other students are unlikely to need them?
- timetable all the necessary dates and times?
- ask other people to advise on resources?

Complete the box below in the usual way. In column 1 enter the actions you plan to take. In column 2 enter the start and finish dates. In column 3 review the effectiveness of your action, together with a note of any further steps you intend to take

Action	Dates	Review

I was glad I'd planned, when I saw the rush for books just before the assignment was due.

UNIT 6

PLANNING YOUR USE OF TIME

What this unit is about

This unit will help you:

→ divide assignments into manageable tasks;

→ identify an outcome for each task;

→ calculate a time for each task;

→ timetable the tasks;

→ draw up a contingency plan.

Time: 1 hour working through the unit, with a further 1 hour 30 minutes for the project.

Resources: file paper; a diary; a pencil and rubber (to amend your plan as necessary).

This unit lies at the heart of time planning. You divide big tasks into smaller ones, to make them manageable. Then you put them into the best order. For each task you define an **outcome** – something you will show for your work. Achieving these does wonders for your confidence! You work out how much time to allow for each task. Finally, you need an alternative plan in reserve, in case anything goes wrong.

The method works for any task. But you are encouraged to choose an assignment, preferably one you are working on, or soon will be. This could be the assignment you used in previous units. You should have the following information on the assignment:

■ its title;

■ the submission date for the assignment and a rough plan of how you will get there (see Unit 3);

■ information (listed in Unit 4) on what an effective answer should be like;

■ the resources you will need and when you will need them (see Unit 5).

You will learn the skills only by trying them out for real, several times. I work through an example during the unit, to show you how the process works.

Stage 1: Identify the goal

The first stage is to be very clear about your goal. In this case, the goal is to complete your assignment.

Project

Write down the title of the assignment you have decided to tackle. Then find out as much as you can about this, as described in Unit 4.

Example

In business studies, students were divided into competing teams. The object was to finish the game in the strongest financial position. Students needed to find out:

● the financial criteria involved;

● how the game would be played, and over what period of time;

● in what form the final report was to be produced;

● how assessment would be carried out.

I shall refer several times to this example in the unit.

Stage 2: Divide the overall job into manageable tasks

In this section you will look at the steps you need to take to achieve your goal of a successfully completed assignment. You will do this first at a general level, and then in more detail.

Project

Decide what rough stages you will need to work through to complete the assignment. You may already have completed this part of your project during your work in Unit 3 and/or Unit 5. If you wish, brainstorm first, using patterned notes. Then put these into a sequence.

Remember that you need only decide on the rough stages through which you plan to take the assignment. You'll break these into more detailed tasks later.

You have taken a very useful planning step, but you need to go further. You have to move from large stages to small and detailed tasks. The following example (the business game assignment) shows the level of detail you have to get to.

Example

This shows the later stages of planning for the business game assignment.

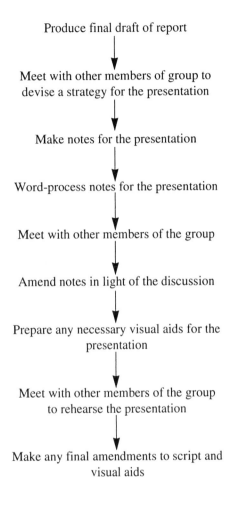

Produce final draft of report

Meet with other members of group to
devise a strategy for the presentation

Make notes for the presentation

Word-process notes for the presentation

Meet with other members of the group

Amend notes in light of the discussion

Prepare any necessary visual aids for the
presentation

Meet with other members of the group
to rehearse the presentation

Make any final amendments to script and
visual aids

The secret is to identify each specific single step. This makes it easier to see exactly:

■ how long it will take;

■ when you'll need to schedule it;

■ how much time you'll need to allow to complete it.

You'll also find that it's easier to see your progress as you move from step to step. You can pick up your work easily, see exactly what you have to do and get it done. All this builds your confidence and morale.

Project

Now turn to the rough stages you made for your own assignment. Take each of these and break it into specific tasks.

Then make sure these tasks are in the most logical order.

When you are confident you have all tasks listed, in the best order, draw up a box such as that started below. List your tasks in the left hand column. The purpose of the other columns will be explained later.

Task	Outcome	Duration	Date	Notes

Stage 3:
Identify an outcome for each task

You should now have a list of very specific tasks that have to be carried out to achieve your goal of a successful assignment. Your next step is to write down an outcome for each task. This will direct your effort and give you an immediate measure against which to judge your success.

Example

Here is an extract from the business studies example.

Task	Outcome
Identify relevant databases	List of databases to consult
Book access to on-line databases	Dates in diary
Find the sources	List books, journals, etc. to consult

Project

For each task on your list write down an outcome, i.e. what you should be able to show for your work. Use the planner you drew up earlier, completing the second column. If you have any difficulty, check the task: is it specific enough?

Outcomes for group meetings

Some assignments require you to work as part of a group. It is particularly important to identify purposes and outcomes for group meetings, otherwise you will all waste a lot of time.

Example

In the example, five group meetings are scheduled. The purpose and outcome for the first two are as follows.

Meeting	Purpose	Outcome
First meeting	To agree the approximate content of each section of the report	Each individual has a list of points they will cover
Second meeting	To check that the drafts together form a coherent report	Each individual takes away a list of the amendments they will make to their section

To specify a purpose and outcome makes it more likely that a group will keep to the point and use time productively. It also helps members prepare adequately for the meeting, by bringing the right resources and carrying out the necessary preparatory work. In the case of the first meeting, for example, group members need to produce rough notes on their sections. Being specific about outcomes can act as a spur to productive group work, before, during and after a meeting.

Stage 4: Calculate a time for each task

You then need to establish how long each task will take.

Task	Outcome	Duration	Date	Notes
Identify relevant databases	List of databases to consult	10 mins		
Book access to on-line databases	Dates in diary	10 mins		
Find the sources	List books, journals, etc. to consult	40 mins		

Project

Use the third column in your planner to enter the time you expect each task to take. Leave the final two columns blank; their purpose will be explained later.

Did you find that many of the tasks require only a little time? This is because you have broken large tasks down into small ones. You can thus more easily predict how long the tasks will take.

Stage 5: Timetable the tasks

You can now enter the dates for each task in your diary or planner, as in the example below.

Example

Task	Outcome	Duration	Date	Notes
1. Identify relevant databases	List of databases	10 mins	1/10	Tasks 1–4: important to carry out these steps well in advance so resources are available for later study sessions starting 2/11. Tasks 1–4 will need two visits to library.
2. Book access to databases	Dates in diary	10 mins	1/10	
3. Find sources	List of sources	40 mins	3/10	
4. Book resources	Completed library slips	20 mins	3/10	

When doing this, try to timetable tasks to appropriate times in the day or week. If, for example, you have a long or difficult task to complete:

■ schedule this to a time when you are likely to be fresh;

■ schedule this to a place where you are unlikely to be disturbed;

■ give yourself some other shorter or easier tasks, for variety.

Now decide when you will carry out each of your listed tasks. Use the fourth column in your planner. The detail of your forward planning will depend on how soon you have to work on the assignment. If this is imminent, then include the times as well as the dates. Add any necessary notes in the final column.

Stage 6: A contingency plan

Things have a habit of going wrong. To cater for this you should:

■ allow some slack time within your planning;

■ check the priority of the tasks, in case you have to shorten, or even omit, some of these under pressure.

See Unit 13 for a discussion of the Pareto Principle, which helps you to prioritise.

Example

In the example sufficient slack time has been allowed. If under further pressure, the students could reduce the number of group meetings from five to as few as two. One meeting could be held to plan the report, and a later meeting to rehearse the presentation. It would also be possible to reduce the time spent taking notes from resources. These changes would, however, be made only under pressure, as the quality of the end product could suffer.

Check your timetable. Have you allowed enough slack time?

If you are under pressure, could you save time by:

■ cutting out tasks;

■ simplifying tasks;

■ completing tasks more quickly?.

Conclusion

Detailed planning of the kind set out in this unit may be new to you. It may seem elaborate, even over the top. But it has been found very effective by people who have to pack a lot into their time. You will need to use the method to plan two or three assignments, before you know whether it works for you. Adapt the stages as necessary in light of your experience.

Action plan

Make a note to carry out this action plan when you have practised on several assignments. Draw up a table like the one below.

What lessons have you learned? These should guide your actions, set out in the first column.

Put start and finish dates in the second column. The final column is for you to review your progress and decide what further action you need to take

Action	Dates	Review

It took me a while to get into planning rather than doing. But then I saved a lot of time. I knew in detail what I was trying to achieve.

TACKLING DIFFERENT TIME-SCALES

What this unit is about

This unit will help you:

➜ distinguish between 'controllable' and 'non-controllable' time;

➜ plan for different time-scales;

➜ analyse your current daily use of time;

➜ plan and review your future daily use of time.

This may seem a tough list of objectives. But detailed planning will save you a great deal of time in the end.

Time: approximately 1 hour, with a further 2 hours for the project (plus time spent on the daily log).

Resources: file paper for notes.

Controllable and non-controllable time

Sometimes our time 'is ours'; at other times it is controlled by other people or things. This unit explores these two types of time. First, a definition:

Controllable time: time you can control. You decide how you use it.

Non-controllable time: time over which you have little or no control. You have little choice over how you use it.

This unit will help you review your use of the time under your own control. But first try the activity. This will enable you to explore more fully the distinction between the two types of time.

1 List some examples of non-controllable time in your own life.

There are many possibilities, including:

■ compulsory, timetabled lectures or seminars;

■ time to meet basic needs, such as eating, sleeping, washing;

■ time spent travelling;

■ domestic tasks, such as cleaning, ironing and shopping;

■ working in paid employment;

■ medical appointments.

Some activities you simply must attend to, and these take time. Eating, sleeping, washing and dressing are obvious examples. Your course is also likely to require you to attend certain sessions.

It's important to note, though, that you do have some influence even over time that is apparently non-controllable.

Can you suggest how time spent on non-controllable activities could be reduced? Take one or two examples from the list you wrote down in response to the first activity.

Some possibilities are perhaps obvious, but still worth considering.

■ Sleeping: you could reduce the hours you spend asleep, either for a short period (for example to complete an assignment) or longer term.

■ Eating: a meal can take anything from ten minutes to three hours!

■ Cleaning: you could leave this for a while, or get someone else to do it for you.

It's sometimes possible to use your non-controllable time for study. You could, for example, listen to language tapes while travelling or cleaning the house.

You need to concentrate, though, on what you do in your controllable time. The project will help you work out how much of this you have at your disposal.

Project

First, choose a typical week in which you would expect to study.

Then complete the table below. Write in the time you would expect to spend on the various non-controllable activities listed. Space has been left to add items particular to you.

Non-controllable activity	Time
Compulsory lectures, seminars, etc.	
Lectures, etc.	
Basic needs (sleeping, eating, etc.)	
Travel time	
Domestic tasks	
Time at work	
Other	
Other	
Other	
Total	

Now add up these hours, using the box provided.

Then deduct your total from 168 (the total hours in the week). This shows you how much controllable time is at your disposal. This is time you decide how to spend.

3 What can you do with this controllable time?

- Some study sessions will have to come from this total. You may have listed reading set books, carrying out projects, preparing assignments.
- Social life (chatting, parties, films, pubs)
- Sport and leisure
- Hobbies
- Watching television
- Visiting family and friends

Think back to the previous activity. How did you react when you saw the total controllable hours at your disposal? Students are often surprised at how little time in fact exists. The exercise is useful partly because it shows how precious is the time you can control. Too precious to waste, for example by:

- looking for things you have lost;
- interruptions you wish would go away;
- pottering around, unable to settle down to work.

These unwelcome activities (covered in Units 8, 9 and 10) have the effect of turning controllable time into non-controllable time. You would not choose to spend your time in these unproductive ways. The ideal is to use time positively, whether in study or in some other activity.

Project

You have now tried out a method for calculating the time you have available in a week. Use the same steps to work out how much controllable time is available tomorrow. Later in this unit you will practise slotting study tasks into this controllable time.

Working over different time-scales

You need to work over longer time-scales than a day or a week. Let's develop this in relation to your course as a whole (see Unit 2).

Example

You are studying a module that lasts for 12 weeks. This is defined as 360–400 study hours. For 10 of these weeks you attend timetabled sessions, occupying approximately 15 hours per week (i.e. a total of 150 hours). In the final two weeks you are expected to use the lecture time for private study (another 30 hours). Thus 180 hours of your study time is already timetabled. This leaves you with 180–220 study hours of your own.

During this time you are expected to:

● prepare three assignments;

● prepare for work in seminars;

● follow up lectures by reading and taking notes;

● carry out other work set by your tutors.

You thus need to find around 200 study hours in total during the 12 weeks. If you are cautious you might make this around 240, to allow some leeway. So on average about 20 hours each week from your controllable time has to be allocated to study.

If you are becoming well organised you will plan at the beginning of a study module. This will include:

■ writing down what you have to achieve (a key task in the above example is to complete the three assignments);

■ drawing up a detailed timetable that will enable you to achieve it.

You translate your goals into specific tasks, each with an outcome and an allocated period of time. You insert these tasks into your controllable time. You thus work from the big picture to the small. Units 2 to 6 cover these and related activities.

Project

Take next week as an example. What priority study tasks do you hope to achieve? What will the outcome of each of these be? How much time will each take? Timetable these tasks into your week.

Planning Documents

You might need some stationery to carry out some of this planning. Unit 12 describes some of the systems commercially available. But the paperwork can be very simple, as set out below.

Example

Your year plan could be on a blank sheet of paper, with a space for your main study goals and for other more personal goals (such as to learn to word process; to save for a holiday; to exercise more).

Your term planner could be another sheet of paper, enabling you to translate your year goals into suitable objectives for the term.

Your month planner could be a bit more detailed, with space for what you hope to achieve over the month.

Your weekly planner could look like this:

Time	Sun	Mon	Tues	Wed	Thurs	Fri	Sat
AM							
PM							
Eve							

Or it could be broken into hourly sessions.

Your day planner could be more detailed again, maybe divided into half-hourly slots.

Planning each day is particularly important. The next section suggests some ways of doing this.

Your daily use of time

Before you can work on improving your daily use of time you need to know how you currently spend your days. The best way to find out is to keep a time log for at least two typical days – weekdays – one after the other. This requires you to write down every 15 minutes what you are doing. This may seem elaborate, but it will give you the data you need to analyse your current use of time. An alternative is to think back over the previous day and to recreate how you spent time then. The problem with this is that you may deceive yourself. The project sets both methods out, so you can choose.

Project

Choose one of the following two methods, to find out how you are currently using time. (Remember that Method 1 is likely to be much more accurate.)

Method 1

Take the next typical day. At 15 minute intervals write down whatever you are doing. Begin when you wake up. You must be honest! It may be a good idea to explain to your friends what you are doing, otherwise they might be puzzled! Your log will look something like this:

10.45: In lecture

11.00: Coffee

11.15: Coffee

11.30: Library, to check references

Method 2

Recall how you spent your time yesterday. Note down what you were doing at 15 minute intervals, as in Method 1 above.

Analysing your log

You can now analyse your daily use of time. Return to your completed log to tackle the next stage of your project.

Project

Look first at your non-controllable time:

■   How much time was outside your control?

■   Could you have decreased this non-controllable time?

Now turn to the time directly under your own control:

■   Had you previously drawn up plans on the use of this time?

■   If so, did you achieve what you set out to do?

■   Did some tasks take longer than you planned? Why?

■   Were some tasks difficult to make a start on?

■   Were you interrupted? If so, why?

■   Could you have avoided/curtailed these interruptions?

■   What was the longest time you spent on a task?

■   Did you spend time during the day planning (e.g. for the next day)?

Imagine this was a friend's day. Given your analysis, what advice would you give the friend on how to manage their time better?

Here are some comments from other students who have carried out this activity.

My 'free' time seemed to get eaten up by one or other member of my family.

I spent ages in the computer centre, but I didn't have much to show for it.

I seem to have spent hours socialising.

It took me 45 minutes to find the right book in the library. But then I had to go to a lecture.

Have you identified improvements you would like to make to your daily use of time? Complete the action plan.

Action plan

What three changes will you introduce to your daily time management?

Your work on the project should give you ideas.

I need to agree with my family times when I can be 'protected', so I can get on without interruptions.

I need to work out exactly what I want to get from my time in the computer centre and focus on that.

I must keep my coffee breaks to 15 minutes maximum.

Here are extracts from the action plans of other students.

Planning and reviewing your day

Before each day you should ideally plan what you intend to do. First, block in your committed time (lectures, travelling, etc.).

Then:

- List the tasks you want to work on in your controllable time (consult your weekly plan if necessary).

- Set an outcome for each task.

- Set an estimated time for each.

- Prioritise the tasks in order.

- Put the tasks into appropriate time slots within the day.

- Put demanding tasks into those parts of the day when you work most efficiently.

- Allow some time for the unexpected.

- Allow some slack time.

You should use a pencil, so you can change your plan as necessary. A much-changed plan can be a sign that you are actually using it. Each day tends to contain the unexpected, requiring you to decide whether or not to continue your pre-set timetable.

Reviewing your day

Get into the habit of reviewing your day as soon as it is over. This will help you check your time estimates and identify possible improvements to your time management. Reviewing need take no more than 15 minutes, at the end of the day. The checklist suggests some questions you can ask yourself.

Checklist

- What did I achieve? (Praise yourself for this!)

- What did I fail to achieve? These items may need to be moved on to the next day's list.

- Why did I fail to achieve these items? Did other more important things crop up? Was I too optimisitic?

- Did the various tasks take roughly the time I had allowed? If not, why not? Do I need to allow more time for such tasks?

- Did I revise my plan as I went through the day?

- Were the changes I made to the plan justified?

- Did I under- or over-estimate my controllable time?

- Did I allocate difficult jobs to times when I was fresh?

- What improvements to my daily time management will I now make?

Project

This project is designed to help you consolidate your work on daily planning.

You can either plan every day in a given period (say a week or 10 days), or plan days

UNIT 8

GETTING DOWN TO WORK

What this unit is about

This chapter will help you:

→ recognise the reasons why you put off work;

→ tackle these delaying tactics.

Time: approximately 30 minutes to work through the chapter and a further 30 minutes planning.

Resources: file paper.

Putting off work is a very common phenomenon, as the following comments show.

> I do just about anything except get on with it. I tidy files, read newspapers, go to the shop, make a snack, have a shower, sew on a button — anything except the work!

> There is always housework. . . And I prefer to talk to my children than get on with studying.

One therapist, Bob Wubbolding, is known to say: 'Whenever I get a new group, I tell them the secret of achieving success as a student. GET STARTED.'

From time to time we all find it difficult to get started. It's all too easy to delay. The trouble is that the task we are putting off does not go away, and the negative feelings, which may include worry and guilt, get worse. On the other hand, if we do tackle the work we benefit from a sense of achievement and renewed energy. This unit will help you get down to your work more quickly and confidently.

Why do you put work off?

This section helps you explore why you put work off. Is there a pattern in your delaying tactics?

1 Start by thinking back to the last time you avoided study. Picture the scene. Then answer the following questions in your notebook.

- What task did you put off?

- What did you do instead?

- What was your excuse?

- What were the results?

I answered this activity as follows:

- The task was writing this book.

- What I did instead were more immediate, smaller and less demanding tasks, such as writing letters and filing.

- My excuse was that I would first get the smaller jobs out of the way, to clear the way for the longer, more important task.

- The result was that I got behind in my timetable and felt stressed. The smaller jobs could all have waited.

Is there a pattern to your delaying?

The incident you recalled in the previous activity may or may not have been typical. You need to see if there is a pattern to your delaying. The next activity should help you with this.

2 Think back over a number of occasions when you have delayed. The questions are similar to those you answered before. But your responses this time should uncover any pattern.

1 What types of job do you put off? Some people, for example, find it easy collecting information for an essay but they delay writing the first draft.

(continued overleaf)

> **2 What do you tend to do instead?**
>
>
>
> **3 What excuses do you generally make for putting these jobs off?**
>
>
>
> **4 What are the results?**

Here is an analysis of the responses other students made to these questions.

1. Types of task:

■ tasks the individual doesn't like;

■ tasks the individual sees as difficult;

■ tasks requiring visits to other places, such as the library;

■ tasks requiring the collection of a number of different resources, such as books, articles, interview data, visits;

■ tasks that seem ill defined, so it's not immediately clear exactly what's wanted.

2. Things done instead:

■ more immediate but less important tasks;

■ smaller jobs;

■ pottering about, wasting time and worrying;

■ day-dreaming;

■ 'fun' things, especially those those which help the individual to forget the main tasks;

■ allowing interruptions to take place.

3. Excuses:

■ I can always do it later when. . . I feel fresher/I have all the resources to hand/I've got the book from the library (etc.);

■ it's boring;

■ I've got better things to do;

■ I don't know where to start and so I may waste my time;

■ I'll get the other things out of the way first.

4. Results:

■ the work is still there;

■ you miss the deadline;

■ you complete it in a panic.

Tackling the situation

You should by now have found a pattern in your behaviour. This section describes some common situations and possible solutions to these. The common patterns are:

- you find it hard to get stuck in to the work;
- something more attractive is immediately available;
- you are bored with the work;
- the next step is not clear;
- the task seems too difficult;
- there are other things to do first;
- you're so far behind that there seems little point;
- you always get interrupted.

You can either work through the whole of this section, or tackle only those patterns that apply to you. The purpose of the section is to help you draw up a specific plan of action to put right whatever is holding you back.

You find it hard to get stuck in to the work

3 Before reading on, what advice would you give to someone with this problem?

One tip is to do all you can to make it likely that you will want to carry on with your work. Study tasks are usually ongoing: you have to pick up something you put down earlier, in a previous study session. It's much more likely that you will want to pick it up if:

- you leave the task at an interesting stage;
- you leave it knowing exactly what has to be done next;
- you know you can do it;
- you make a brief note, to remind yourself of the next stage and how long this should take.

Something more attractive is immediately available

4 Again, what advice would you give to someone with this problem?

Unfortunately, something more attractive usually *is* available! Nevertheless, you could:

- remind yourself of the importance of your study task.

- remove the alternative attractions (the newspaper, the CD or whatever).

- study in a place where the distractions simply are not present. You cannot, for example, watch television in a library.

- promise yourself the attraction when you have finished the task, or a defined part of it – i.e. reward yourself with it.

You are bored with the work

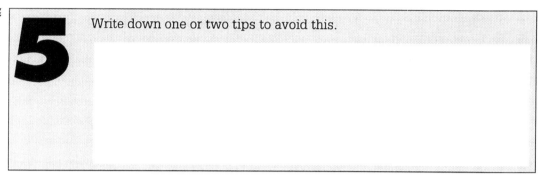

Write down one or two tips to avoid this.

Look back to the advice given for the first situation, i.e. leave the previous study session at an interesting stage.

Here are some other tips:

- Keep several tasks running in parallel (see Unit 3). At least one of these should be at a stage that interests you.

- Remind yourself of the positive reasons for getting the work done. These will be the reasons that particularly motivate you.

See also the points made under the next two headings.

The next step is not clear

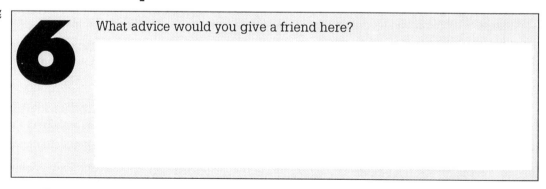

What advice would you give a friend here?

- Tease out several possible next steps. Choose one and see where it leads.

- Ask another student, or a tutor, for advice on the next step.

- Leave a study session with a clear next step. You can then resume easily.

The task seems too difficult

- Some of the earlier advice applies here. You can avoid the situation by leaving the previous study session at a high point.

- Work out exactly where the difficulty lies. Ask for help. Note: people can help you only if you can be precise about the difficulty (see Unit 12).

- Break the task into small specific steps, each with a clear outcome (see Unit 6). Tackle these steps, and note your success.

- Remind yourself of other times when you have succeeded. This should boost your confidence in your ability, and release energy.

There are other things to do first

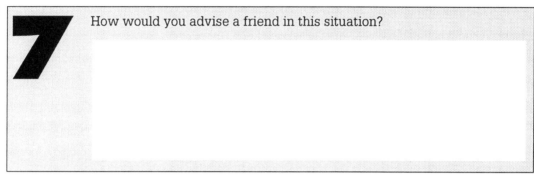

7 How would you advise a friend in this situation?

You might ask whether these 'other things' really are pressing, or are they just excuses. Will they wait?

It often helps to list such activities and arrange times to carry them out later.

You're so far behind that there seems little point

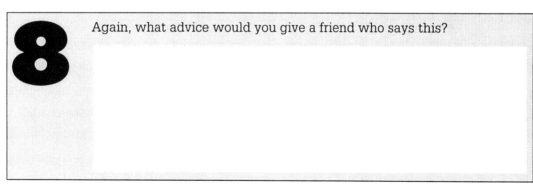

8 Again, what advice would you give a friend who says this?

This sounds like desperation point. This attitude can end only in the failure to do anything at all. The advice you would give depends on the seriousness of the situation. At one extreme, radical action may be needed, such as transferring to another course. If the situation is less serious, the first point to make is that to do something, however small, is better than to do nothing.

The advice to break up the task into small steps is useful: the individual can then see progress in specific achievements, one after the other. At the same time, the student might be able to negotiate an extension to a deadline; you will find guidance on this in Unit 11.

You always get interrupted

This is covered in Unit 9.

Conclusion

Some advice applies generally, whatever your specific situation. The checklist below draws your attention to points of good practice.

Checklist

Have I:

- broken the job down into smaller tasks?

- set specific targets?

- measured whether I have reached the targets?

- left work at an interesting and manageable stage at the end of each study session?

- sought help from other people?

- removed or avoided sources of distraction?

- started work promptly?

- tackled the important work?

Action plan

This gives you the opportunity to plan how you will tackle your own delaying tactics. Your work on the activities earlier in the unit will help you.

Draw up and complete a plan under the following headings:

- Type of delay: write in the type(s) of delay you wish to tackle. If there are several, put them into order of importance.

- Proposed action: describe what you will do to tackle each type of delay.

- Dates: give the dates for starting and completing the action.

- Review: complete this column when you have had a chance to carry out the action and assess how effective it has been. Use this column to write in any further action you propose to take.

UNIT 9

CONTROLLING INTERRUPTIONS

What this unit is about

This unit will help you:

→ identify typical interruptions that stop you working;

→ work out the reasons for these interruptions;

→ tackle the interruptions that prevent you making progress.

Time: approximately 30 minutes to work through the unit, and a further 30 minutes planning.

Resources: file paper.

The Concise Oxford Dictionary defines 'to interrupt' as 'to prevent from proceeding continuously. . . to break continuity'. This puts it exactly. You are making progress on a study task when someone or something stops you. Unit 8 dealt with the problem of not getting started; this unit helps you handle interruptions to your progress once you are underway.

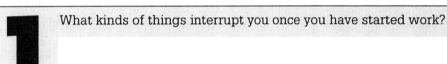

1   What kinds of things interrupt you once you have started work?

You might have included some of the following points:

■ social life, for example someone suggests you join them at the pub/at a party;

■ telephone calls;

■ family commitments, for example putting the children to bed;

■ domestic activity, for example having to shop, cook;

■ employment, for example having to get to work at set times;

■ illness;

■ friends who need your help;

■ partner/boyfriend/girlfriend demands your time.

Interruptions

These interruptions can be divided into several common types.

1   Something more attractive turns up to tempt you from your work.

2   An accident or emergency requires you to act urgently.

3   Something you feel you ought to do stops you working.

The following activity will help you recognise each type of interruption and what causes it.

Read the scenarios below. Each illustrates one of the three types of interruption listed above. Complete the box for each scenario, entering 1, 2 or 3 to show what kind of interruption it represents.

Scenario	Type	Scenario	Type	Scenario	Type
(a)		(c)		(e)	
(b)		(d)		(f)	

(a)   You are working at home, writing up the lab report on an experiment you carried out earlier that day. The phone rings. It's your father – your mother has been taken ill and is in hospital. He thinks you should return at once, to see her.

(b)   You go to the library to make a start on a long-overdue essay. You are getting stuck in when a friend appears. She tells you about a party about to be held in a friend's flat just down the road. Lots of people will be there. The host is recovering from depression and the party should cheer him up. You will meet several friends just back from a field trip. You'll have a good time.

(c)   You are at home, reading a unit of a recommended textbook. Thoughts of things you really should do keep distracting you. You need some extra ingredients for tonight's meal; the bath needs cleaning; a visitor is arriving in three days' time for the weekend, and you have to tidy their room.

(d)   You are in the library, making good progress on a project. You reckon that in the two hours left before lunch you will have caught up on your timetable. Your heart sinks as you see John coming towards you. He'll be asking for help on his assignment, as he knows you did a similar task last term. You don't want to hurt his feelings.

(e)   You are well underway with your poster design, a task you must complete tonight. The phone goes. It's your best friend ringing for a chat. This usually takes at least an hour.

(f)   You are summarising the results of a survey you carried out on attitudes to benefits payments. You are doing this on the train back from a visit to your partner. When you get back to your flat you plan to prepare overhead projector acetates for your contribution to the group presentation on the following day. The train comes to an unexpected halt. The senior conductor announces that the train will be seriously delayed. You will not arrive in time to prepare the acetates.

Your table should look like the one below.

Scenario	Type	Scenario	Type	Scenario	Type
(a)	2	(c)	3	(e)	1
(b)	1	(d)	3	(f)	2

(a)   This is clearly an accident/emergency situation.

(b)   This is an example of something more attractive turning up. Admittedly, the friend is recovering from depression, which might tempt you to put this in category 3 (you feel you ought to go). But the main motive here seems to be to have a good time with friends. Since plenty of people are going, your absence is unlikely to make much difference. You could presumably see the friends recently returned from a field trip some other time.

(c)   An example of 3: things you feel you should do. None of these seems immediately necessary. Some food is already available, you need only extras. Cleaning the bath could wait, and there's plenty of time to tidy the room so it's ready for the weekend visit.

(d)   Another example of 3. You feel you ought to help the friend.

(e)   Another example of 1: something more attractive turning up. The telephone is a common and insistent interruption!

(f)   The planned work cycle has been interrupted for reasons beyond your control. The delayed train is an 'accident': you could not reasonably have expected it – though you could have taken some alternative work to do, just in case. . .

Now turn to your own experience of interruptions. Through the project, you can collect evidence on the types of interruptions you meet, and what causes them.

Project

Over the next few days keep a log of the occasions when you are interrupted. Note down:

■   when the interruption took place (time);

■   where the interruption took place;

■   what type of interruption each was;

■   how much time you lost;

■   what you were doing before the interruption and after it.

Draw up a table for your log, using the main headings above.

Also note down interruptions you resisted. How did you achieve this?

Read on when you have completed your log.

Now review the results.

Check your log, to see whether there's a pattern.

■   Are you interrupted regularly at the same times?

■   Are you interrupted regularly in a particular place?

■   Are you vulnerable to any particular types of interruption?

■   Are you regularly interrupted when you are working on difficult study tasks?

Also check your log to find out:

■ how much time each interruption cost you;

■ how much time in total you lost through interruptions.

The project will give you more information about your behaviour. This information will help you to draw up your action plan.

Tackling interruptions

The examples we looked at earlier in the unit show that interruptions differ according to the degree of influence or control you have over them. The examples in fact fall along a continuum, as shown below.

◄───►

(b) and (c)	(c) and (d)	(a) and (f)
under your		not under
control		your control

Look at scenarios (b), (c), (d) and (e). For each, recommend an action you could take to keep working, i.e. to overcome the interruption.

(b) You could overcome this by reviewing your priorities and deciding that in this case work is more important than pleasure. You could act assertively and tell your friend that you want to continue working. If necessary you could add to this, for example by saying you will make contact with the host over the next couple of days.

(c) Again, you could review your priorities and decide that the other activities can be postponed to some other time.

(d) You could politely but assertively explain that you have to carry on working. If you wish, you could fix a time to meet John later. You can also, of course, limit the amount of help you decide to give.

(e) Again, you could point out to your friend that you are too busy to chat just now. You could go on to say that you will ring back the following evening, setting a time if that would help.

It's also possible to have at least some influence over unforeseen interruptions. You can, for example:

■ build some slack time into the timetable;

■ have alternative strategies ready in case of interruption. In our earlier example (f) you could have taken some reading on the train, as well as the acetates.

So in most cases you do have a degree of control over whether or not to give way to interruptions. As the student comments below show, you can act to reduce the number or length of interruptions. In practice we often do give way, trying to persuade ourselves that we have a good reason. We blame someone (or something) from stopping us when what we are really doing is interrupting ourselves. Frequently giving in to interruptions is a sign of poor motivation or poor self-management.

I close the door and won't answer it if I'm working. My friends know this.

I work in another place, out of the way, where no-one knows I am.

If I am interrupted I look at my watch and give a maximum of ten minutes for the break from work.

I use a kitchen timer. When it rings I always return immediately to my study.

Prioritising

You will notice the frequent use of the phrase 'priorities'. When faced with conflicting courses of action you have to decide which has top priority. One way to do this is to carry out a quick analysis of the costs and benefits of the different courses of action. In the party example (b) the benefit is short term: a good time meeting friends. But there's a longer term cost: the work doesn't get done and the individual gets stressed as a result. You'll often have to make speedy calculations of this kind.

Assertiveness

I have several times mentioned the need for assertive behaviour in limiting the potential damage interruptions can cause. But what exactly is 'assertive behaviour'? To be 'assertive' is to express your own needs and feelings straightforwardly, honestly and without anxiety.

How does an assertive person differ from (a) someone who is non-assertive and (b) someone who is aggressive?

(a) The non-assertive person behaves passively and has difficulty in standing up for him- or herself.

(b) The aggressive person expresses his or her needs in a way which puts down or humiliates others.

Do you need to behave more assertively? If so, you may find the following checklist helpful.

Checklist

Do I:

- openly state my own needs and opinions?

- make my feelings clear?

- say 'no' when necessary?

- say 'I don't understand' when necessary?

- make it clear to others when I want to work?

- feel comfortable about saying I want to be left alone?

- feel comfortable about making mistakes?

- feel comfortable about changing my mind?

If you need help in becoming more assertive, see the Further Reading list on page 96.

Conclusion

As you should now see, a lot depends on how you behave. If you want to control interruptions you need to be assertive on occasions. Otherwise, your time will never be your own. It will be controlled by other people. (See Unit 7 for more on 'non-controllable' time.) You also need to be consistent. Once friends see you mean what you say, they will show more respect for your time.

One student said: 'Interruptions are always welcome if you dislike the work involved.' This brings us back to the key importance of motivation: making sure you are on the right course and can see the point of the work you are asked to undertake.

You should now be ready to complete your action plan.

Action plan

Complete a plan like the one below as follows:

- Situation: write in the type of interruption you want to tackle.

- Proposed action: describe what you will do to tackle the interruption.

- Dates: give the dates for starting and finishing the action.

- Review: complete this column when you have had a chance to see how effective you have been in carrying out your plan. Use this column to write in any further action you decide to carry out.

Situation	Proposed action	Dates	Review

UNIT 10

ORGANISING YOUR WORKING ENVIRONMENT

What this unit is about

This unit will help you:

➔ identify improvements you could make to all aspects of your working environment;

➔ plan to carry out these improvements;

➔ manage your study in a range of different environments, including some that are less than perfect.

Time: approximately 60 minutes to work through the unit, with a further 60 minutes planning.

Resources: file paper.

Studying is difficult enough. Too often students have additional complications because the environment in which they work is unsuitable. Some of these difficulties you may have to live with; others you can do something about. This unit looks first at the room in which you usually work. The focus then shifts to your immediate workspace – desk or table, drawers. Later sections cover studying in different places within your institution, on the move and in inconvenient locations.

The aim of the unit is to help you make the most of all the different places in which you choose to (or have to) study. The result should be that you can get down to work more quickly and waste less time.

The room you usually work in

Most students have to work for at least some of the time in a 'private' space – their room. Ideally, what should this be like, if it's to encourage study?

1 Make notes on your ideal study room. Consider:

■ space

■ heat

■ light (natural/artificial)

■ absence of noise

■ power

■ work surfaces

(continued overleaf)

- shelving
- storage facilities
- equipment
- stationery

Here are some comments from other students:

I use different places. The kitchen is warm, but too near food and drink distractions. The bedroom is good for relaxed reading, but there's no table and it's not very warm. Ideally I'd like a mixture: somewhere warm, with space to be able to lounge while reading and access to a good-sized table.

I put all my make up away and use the dressing table; no-one touches that!

The Ideal Room

Different students have different preferences. So no one learning environment will please everybody. Most students need quiet in order to concentrate, but you will easily find people who prefer to work to background music, or even in a room in which conversations are taking place.

Generally, though, the following features are helpful:

- Reasonable space, so you can sit comfortably at a table or desk.
- A decent-sized worktop on which you can spread papers.
- A comfortable chair in which to read and relax.
- Storage spaces in or near to the desk.
- Shelves for books, etc.
- A ventilated room the right temperature for study (maximum 20°C).
- Peace and quiet when you need it.
- Natural light, with good general additional lighting, e.g. from a fluorescent tube.
- Absence of distractions.
- Convenient power points for computer, audiocassette recorder, etc.
- Equipment you need, e.g. computer, drawing board.
- Adequate stationery – pens, pencils, highlighter, paper, files binders, etc.

Look at your response to Activity 1. In light of the discussion, do you want to add anything to your description of the ideal room? Amend your list of features as necessary.

You should now have a list of ideal features. The project will help you check what is actually available in your situation. This will show how big the gap is between the ideal and the current reality. You can then decide what action to take.

Project

Look at your own workspace. For each item on your list give your workspace a score ranging from 0 (completely fails to provide this item) up to 5 (excellent provision of this item). Add any notes.

Here is an extract from another student's response to this activity.

Lighting – 0 (Lighting poor; small, dim central light and awkward-to-use table lamps)

Quiet – 4 (Very peaceful, apart from occasional faint noises from next door)

Power points – 1 (Poorly positioned sockets, and not many of them)

Warmth – 2 (Difficult to warm the room without it becoming stuffy)

The action plan at the end of this unit will help you improve your main work room. Anything on your list scoring 2 or less probably needs attention. Some changes will be cheap and easy to attend to, others less so. Alternatives are usually available, for example buying a multi-point lead is cheaper and easier than putting in more power sockets.

Your work surface

You now need to look at your more immediate working area, and especially the space on which you usually study.

3 Look at your worktop. It may be a desk or a table. Draw it, i.e. showing all the things that are currently on it. Don't rearrange it before you begin!

Then answer these questions (honestly!):

Is the space clear for working on?

Can you easily find the things you need for work (pens, paper, etc.)?

Do you have reserve supplies of stationery, etc.?

If the space is meant to work on, it should be clear of items other than those which you are actually using. A clear surface invites you to work.

You should bring out (for example from a drawer) the papers relating to your current task, and make a prompt start. When you've finished, you should remove the papers.

Desks should be used for working, not eating or drinking.

You should be able to find easily all the tools and stationery you need, including computer disks if appropriate.

Other items of stationery should be easily available but not actually on the workspace (spare pen, adhesive tape, cartridges, scissors, glue, spare disks, etc.). These could be in a desk drawer.

Books should be on a nearby shelf, not piled on the desk top.

Now review your own workspace against these points. Give yourself a score from 0 (a poor performance on the item) to 5 (excellent) on each of the following:

- desk space is clear;
- immediately needed stationery is available;
- reserve stationery is available nearby (not on desktop);
- resources (books, etc.) are nearby (not on desktop);

On what points do you need to take action?

My own desktop is shown below. It scores low (1) on 'clear desk space'. So it's obvious where I should act. I need to remove all the papers not needed for my current activity. I'm currently using the desk as a store rather than as a worksurface.

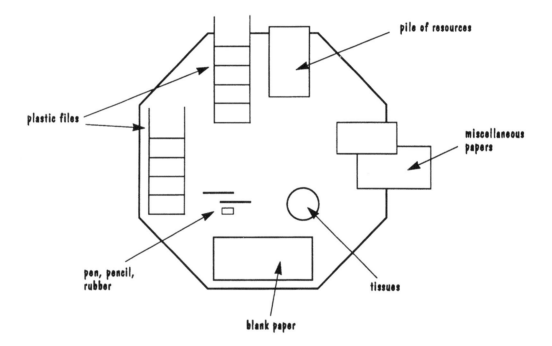

This section has once again described what is normally considered good practice. Some students do manage to produce good work from a muddled desk. They succeed, however, in spite of the muddle, not because of it. Only you can decide whether or not you need to change your current habits. But if you lose things regularly, get annoyed at the muddle, knock papers off your desk trying to create space, rarely have the right equipment to hand – these are all signs that you are not working efficiently. To rearrange your workspace could well remove these sources of irritation. Many changes are simple to carry out but make life much easier. These are the kinds of change you need to look for in all your time management.

Managing your computer desktop

Students are increasingly expected to use computers, for example:

■   to access information;

■   to manipulate spreadsheets and databases;

■   to present finished assignments.

Familiarity with computers and associated software is thus increasingly important. You may be fortunate in having your own personal computer. More probably, you use machines within your institution, for example in a computer workshop or the library.

Modern software puts another workspace at your disposal: the 'desktop' on the machine. By pulling down **menus**, opening **windows**, manipulating **icons**, you carry out the electronic equivalent of the processes we discussed earlier. You can open files, move them around, store them, organise them into folders, weed them out every so often.

In some ways the computer makes life much easier. Some machines, for example, have a 'find' facility which saves you time searching. (How often have you wished you had such a facility when looking for bits of paper in your other files!)

But to get full benefit from a computer you have to be systematic, especially if you are using a shared machine. Otherwise you will lose your work and waste time. Familiarise yourself fully with the operation of software you are using, and with any systems in place within your institution.

Label all your disks clearly. You may, for example, need: file title, programme used, your name and phone number, the date when you last entered the data. Make sure you label different versions of the same document, otherwise you may send your tutor an uncorrected version of an assignment. Keep a library of your disks as carefully as you would store books or papers.

Ask yourself the following questions.

Checklist

Have I:

●   named files clearly;

●   stored files and folders logically;

●   set aside a short time each week for putting the desktop in order;

●   set aside a short time each month for throwing out old files;

●   labelled floppy disks clearly;

●   made daily back-ups of working files;

●   labelled different versions of the same document.

Handling paper

Ideally you have on your desk only those papers relating to the project on which you are currently working. This section considers what you do with all the other papers you need for studying. Students often have to manage large quantities of paper, including notes from books, assignments, photocopies of articles, handouts. This can grow to an unmanageable pile. The next activity helps you assess whether you need to improve your paper management.

 Answer yes (Y) or no (N) to the following questions:

Have you lost any papers recently?

Have you spent time hunting for papers, books, etc.?

Do you get depressed by all the papers you have to deal with?

Is it more than a month since you went through your papers and threw some out?

If you answered yes to any of the questions perhaps you should review the way you handle paper. The checklist below should help. Later, you will be invited to decide which points you could build into your action plan.

Checklist

Do I:

- keep together all the papers relating to one activity or assignment?
- regularly check the order of papers in my files?
- weed out my papers regularly (weekly, monthly, termly)?
- review my methods for storing and classifying notes (see the tables below)?

Ways of storing notes

This table compares some of the commoner ways of storing notes.

Method	Implications
Loose-leaf folders	Easy to subdivide and add to later.
Ring binder	Also easy to add to: sheets less likely to fall out. Material could be kept in plastic pockets.
Filing cards	Easy to shuffle and reorganise. Good for project, essay or report plans.
Notebook	Convenient to carry. Pages cannot fall out.
Concertina file	Has ready-made subdivisions.
Wordprocessor	Easy to edit material and to reuse for other writing. Remember to make back-up copies.
Tape recorder	Good if you find it easier to say things than write them down. Useful for recording speech too.

Ways of classifying notes

Within your filing system, you need to organise your notes so you can find them again.

Method	Implications
By date	May be useful for a series of lectures. You may forget when you made notes, though.
By first letter	A simple system to use. May let you down if you make a lot of notes.
By topic	Often the best system as it is easy to add to as you go along. But you need to choose topics that are easy to file under.
A mixture	For example, alphabetically within topics.

Source: Freeman and Meed, *How to Study Effectively*, Collins Educational/NEC, 1993

I make sure I throw out more paper each week than I actually take in during that time.

I colour code my papers, e.g. everything relating to project A has a red sticker in the top left hand corner, project B has a yellow sticker.

Making the most of the facilities your institution provides

Your institution will provide a range of facilities. These could include libraries, computer centres, common rooms, lecture and seminar rooms (when not in use); learning centres; seats outside (when the weather is fine). Such facilities are useful in a number of ways:

- for private study (for example, the library);
- for group work (for example, a seminar room);
- for access to resources (for example, an open learning centre).

Each facility will also have disadvantages. You may have to book in advance (see Unit 5), for example, or some places may be noisy.

If you are studying by open learning your resources may be more limited. But you may be able to negotiate access to your nearest college, or to other local facilities.

The action plan will prompt you to become more aware of the facilities open to you and how you can gain access to them.

Studying on the move

Students are often mobile, travelling both short and long distances. You probably use different forms of transport: train, bus, car, bike, foot. Travelling is often 'dead' time. But, with forethought, different types of journey can be used productively for different study purposes, as the examples below show.

The action plan at the end of this unit asks you to consider whether you make the maximum use of the time you spend travelling.

> I can't read on the bus — the constant stopping and starting makes me feel sick. But I use bus travel to think through how I will answer my assignments.

> When travelling by car I play audiocassettes of programmes related to my course, and language tapes.

> I find the train ideal for getting reading done.

> I plan my week as I'm jogging.

Studying in uncongenial environments

You often have to study in circumstances that are less than perfect, for example:

■ in crowded libraries;

■ in shared study bedrooms;

■ on the move between sites;

■ in noisy, inconvenient places.

In addition, you may have to carry your books and files around with you, without being able to store them in a locker.

In circumstances such as these you need to plan very carefully, for example:

■ thinking through in advance exactly what resources you need to take with you;

■ selecting tasks that you can study with lightweight resources, or for very short periods.

Again, the action plan will help you consider this aspect of your environment.

Conclusion

Every student is different. While this unit has given what would generally be considered good advice, you need to experiment, to find out what works for you. Where one student needs the absolute quiet of a college chapel, another studies in the coffee bar on Euston Station, because he likes the noise!

Through experimentation, you should be able to:

● adjust your regular working environment better to suit your style;

● organise your desk and storage space more effectively;

● make the most of the facilities provided by your institution;

● plan, so that you can work in environments that are less than perfect.

Not only do you need to experiment, you also need to reflect on what you do, and decide on your next steps on the path to better self-management.

Action plan

This will help you plan the actions you need to take on all the aspects of your study environment covered in this unit. Follow the headings suggested for your plan.

Your room

What action will you take to improve the room in which you work?

> Action:
>
> Date:
>
> Cost:
>
> Review:

Your worksurface

What action will you take to improve your use of your table or desk?

> Action:
>
> Date:
>
> Cost:
>
> Review:

Your computer desktop

What action will you take to:

■ explore the capabilities of your desktop?

■ learn to use the facilities?

■ monitor your progress?

> Action:
>
> Date:
>
> Cost:
>
> Review:

Handling paper

What action will you take to improve your management of paper?

Action:

Date:

Cost:

Review:

Facilities in your institution

What action will you take to:

■ find out the facilities available in your institution;

■ find out the facilities available in your community;

■ find out how to gain access to these facilities;

■ ensure you use these facilities to the full?

Action:

Date:

Cost:

Review:

Studying on the move

What action will you take to make better use of time you spend travelling: on foot, by bike, on the bus, in the car, on the train?

Mode of travel	Action	Dates	Review
On foot			
By bike			
On the bus			
On the train			
In the car			
Other			

Studying in uncongenial environments

What action will you take to get the most from inconvenient locations and situations?

Location/situation:

Type of study you could undertake:

Date to start:

Date to review progress:

Comments:

UNIT 11

HANDLING TIME STRESS

What this unit is about

This unit will help you:

→ recognise causes and signs of stress;

→ identify those caused by time pressure;

→ manage time-related stress;

→ renegotiate your workload, if necessary.

Time: approximately 45 minutes to work through the unit and a further 30 minutes planning.

Resources: file paper.

Some degree of stress is essential. Too little and we get bored, tired or frustrated. But we all react differently. What to one person is stress, to another is the right level of challenge. Different people find different things stressful. One individual might be a fearless rockclimber but stressed beyond endurance in an exam room. Two people can view exactly the same situation from different perspectives.

When the pressure is about right for us we work effectively, feeling in control. This unit explores stress arising from time and suggest ways of tackling this. But first, what causes stress and how do we recognise it?

Stress

Causes of Stress

A combination of three things can lead to stress: demands you perceive as too exacting, tight constraints and a low level of support. The following activity will help you recognise this combination.

Jean is studying to become a nurse. She is falling behind with her work and missing deadlines. Her mother has become ill and Jean has to visit her most nights. Jean's tutor is unsympathetic; she thinks this is all part of life and that Jean will just have to organise her time better.

Identify: (a) the work demands; (b) the constraints; and (c) the level of support.

(a)

(b)

(c)

This should be reasonably clear:

(a) Jean is missing deadlines on her course.

(b) The constraints are her family circumstances, which make it difficult for Jean to find the time to study.

(c) Jean's tutor is unsympathetic, thus leading to a low level of support.

You'll return to this definition of stress at the end of the unit, to consider which of these three elements can be modified in your own case.

Signs of stress

You can often tell if someone is under stress from the way they behave.

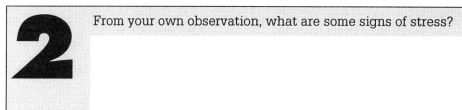
From your own observation, what are some signs of stress?

Stress can be displayed in obvious, external ways – anger, irritability, tears – or in more subtle ways such as withdrawal or depression. People's moods can swing unpredictably when under stress. In terms of study, the stressed individual may overwork frantically or, at the other extreme, do nothing.

Some stress is immediate and shown by signs such as increased heartbeat and sweating. Other stress is long term and is shown more generally, for example by a tendency to escape from responsibility.

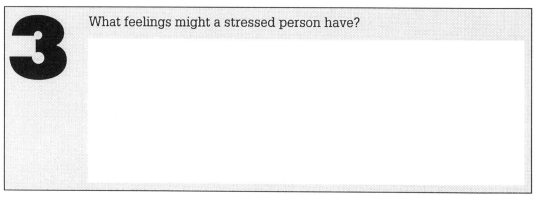
What feelings might a stressed person have?

If you're stressed you can feel anxious, trapped, in a panic. You can feel that things are running out of control, that you are on the edge of a crisis. The smallest complication can throw you out of gear. Stressed individuals often lack confidence, and confidence in your own ability is the key not only to success in study but to many other things as well.

When you're stressed your work often suffers. You feel dissatisfied with what you've done. You can't concentrate; you spend time unproductively; you work inefficiently; you make mistakes. You work slavishly, for example reading every word of books, noting every point.

Physically you can suffer too. Headaches, sleeplessness, indigestion, exhaustion, susceptibility to 'bugs' and accidents: stress can lead to any of these symptoms.

Stress can also induce drug dependence, as individuals try to 'forget themselves'. Excessive smoking, drinking and even television viewing can thus be signs of stress. Stress and an unhealthy lifestyle tend to go together.

> I chew my knuckles. My head feels tight. I glaze over when others are present.

> I get more and more books to read for my assignments. But as soon as I open one, I can't concentrate and I feel sick.

> I get stressed driving to college. I worry about arriving on time. Parking worries me.

Time stress

Stress can be caused by many things. This unit looks at stress that results from the student's perception of time, or rather lack of time. You have first to analyse the causes of time stress in your own particular case. Constructive analysis (not the same as worrying!) will help you resolve any problems.

4 Which of the following situations do you find yourself in? Tick the boxes that most nearly apply to you, then read the relevant comments and suggestions that follow this activity.

1   There's always too much to do. I worry about getting it all done – even having nightmares about it sometimes.

2   I frequently miss deadlines. I can't seem to organise myself to get assignments done on time.

3   I seem to be working all the time, to the detriment of other things.

4   I work hard and put the time in. But I don't seem to get the rewards for my efforts.

1   Is there really 'too much to do' or is this just your own personal view? Are other students stressed in the same way? If so, you may all be suffering from a badly designed study programme. Your tutors may not be liaising over assignment dates. In this case, work through Unit 2 and the section *Handling overload* later in this unit.

You may be facing issues outside your own control, as described in Unit 9. In this case you may need to prioritise and persuade your tutors to extend their deadlines.

Maybe you've fallen behind with your work, for some reason. You may be over-conscientious, a perfectionist. If so, this book can help you, provided you draw up action plans and persist with them. You may need help from friends or a counsellor (see Unit 12).

Alternatively, you may have fallen behind through poor time management. It might be useful to revisit the questions towards the end of Unit 1.

2. Are you planning as carefully as you should? Are you anticipating busy periods and taking action accordingly? (Units 3, 5, 6 and 7 should help you plan more effectively.) Do you need to negotiate more time with your tutor (see *Negotiating workloads* later in this unit).

3. Are you clear as to what your tutors want from you? (See Units 2 and 4.) Do you need to schedule non-work activities (for example social life and exercise) into your timetable? Are you on the right study programme? Are other problems affecting you, such as family or health?

4. Do you set outcomes for your study tasks? Do you identify the tasks that really count? Do you practise the 'Pareto Principle'?

The Pareto Principle

Vilfredo Pareto was a nineteenth-century Italian economist and sociologist. He noticed that the significant items in any group were the smallest, in the ratio 80:20, i.e. 20 per cent of the items were the really important ones. Think how this might apply to everyday things, say a shopping list or a list of domestic tasks: only one out of every five things listed might be really important.

1 Can you rephrase the Pareto Principle so that it applies to how you use your time for study?

2 What implications does the Principle have for your study?

1 The Principle suggests that 20 per cent of your study activities create 80 per cent of your results/achievements (and the other 80 per cent accounts for only 20 per cent of your results).

2 It bears out the need for prioritising. You need to identify the 20 per cent of activities that really count, and concentrate on them. Either drop some of the other 80 per cent, or get them out of the way as quickly as possible. Give your best time and effort to the smaller number of key tasks.

Handling overload

Overload can sometimes result from excessive assessment requirements. In modular courses assignment deadlines can fall awkwardly, all at more or less the same time. But your feeling of overload may be the result of poor time management. This section will help you decide.

Project

To tackle this project you need a clear idea of the work you have to do, and how long you expect this to take. If you are unclear on these two things, see Units 2, 3, 5, 6 and 7.

Follow the steps below to complete this activity.

1   List all the work you have to do in a given time period, such as a month.

2   Estimate how many hours this work will take.

3   How many hours are there in total in the period you are considering? (For a month it is 30 days x 24, i.e. 720 hours.)

4   Calculate the hours you have available for study (see Unit 7 for help with this).

5   Compare this figure with the estimate you wrote down at step 2 above. Have you enough time?

6   If there is a gap, work through the figures again. For example:

   ■ Did you overestimate at step 2?

   ■ Could you use the Pareto Principle to reduce the time you need to do the work?

   ■ Could you create any more study time?

7   If you are still left with a big gap you may need to negotiate your workload (and especially deadlines for assignments) with your tutor. In this case, see the next section.

Negotiating workloads

If you are convinced that your workload is too heavy, consider the possibility of negotiating with your tutor(s). But make sure you do this well before any deadlines, otherwise it will look like an excuse rather than a negotiation. You may be able to achieve:

■ a redefinition of the assignment task(s) to make them more manageable in the time available;

■ an extension to your deadlines.

Use the 'steps for negotiation' set out below.

1   Make sure you have a case. The most obvious way to do this is to ask other students. If they agree, you can approach your tutor(s) as a group.

2   Work out what you want to achieve. This becomes your target. Do you have a fallback position, in case your target is not possible?

3   Consider the person with whom you will be negotiating. What will they want? What might they be prepared to accept?

4   Make a case that will satisfy both you and your tutor(s).

5   Collect the evidence you need to convince your tutor(s). They will need to be reassured that you will be able to achieve the alternative plan you are putting forward.

6   Plan your approach. When is the best time to talk to your tutor(s)? Where? Should you prepare for your meeting, for example by outlining your case in writing first?

The following example is of a negotiation for the first draft of this book. The numbers refer to the stages of negotiation, described above.

Example

I negotiated a later date for sending in the draft manuscript of this book.

My case (see 1 above) was that the delay would enable us to involve students and tutors, at the start of a new term. We could also test out parts of some of the units.

My target date was 1 October, but I had the fallback position of 21 September (2).

I considered the editor with whom I was negotiating. I knew this book was one of three, and that he would have to persuade his boss to accept a later date – one that might make the production process more complicated (3). But I also knew that the case for a better first draft would appeal, as this would mean both a better book and less work at later stages (4).

I carried out a detailed analysis to show that the later date was realistic, and that, short of accidents, I really would be able to deliver the manuscript on that date (5). I realised I had to carry out the negotiation in early July, before the editor left for his two-week holiday on 16 July. I knew he would have to get the agreement of the publishers before setting off.

I wrote first, we then discussed it over the phone, and we agreed on the fallback date of 21 September (6).

Conclusion

At the beginning of this unit we defined the three associated elements of stress: exacting demands, strong constraints and low support. If you feel you might become stressed you can work on one or more of these. Remember you need to *anticipate* stress and take action before it attacks.

You can plan to:

- make the study demands less exacting (for example by redefining an assignment);

- lessen the constraints (for example by creating more time);

- increase the support (for example by getting help from a friend, a tutor or a counsellor).

It will help if you can modify even only one of these three ingredients. The aim is to create just the right amount of stress, so you are stimulated to work effectively.

Action plan

The action plan will help you decide what action to take in the light of this unit. Write notes in answer to these questions:

- Are you currently stressed because of time pressures?

- What are the signs of your stress?

- What are the main causes of the stress?

- What action can you take?

A wide range of possible actions is suggested in this unit, including:

- practising new time management skills;

- negotiating overload;

- carrying out further reading on stress and how to control it;

- talking to other students, a tutor, a counsellor.

Using these suggestions together with ideas of your own, complete a box like the one below, as follows:

● Action: write in the actions you will take.

● Dates: write the start and finish dates.

● Review: use this space to comment on the effectiveness of your plan; add any actions you propose to take next.

Action	Dates	Review

UNIT 12

SOURCES OF HELP

What this unit is about

This unit will help you:

→ list people who can support you in your time management;

→ identify the help each person can give;

→ identify other sources of help, such as diaries, planners and courses;

→ plan to use sources of help relevant to you.

Time: approximately 30 minutes to work through the unit; 1 hour for the projects.

Resources: file paper.

People

The book frequently emphasises the help other people can give in helping you change the way you manage your time.

1 What types of help could a student be given? Complete the sentence:

Someone could help by

Here are some suggestions:

■ discussing possible time management targets;

■ giving encouragement, for example to complete an action plan;

■ explaining what an assignment requires;

■ giving information, for example on where you might find resources quickly;

■ discussing how to plan a group project;

■ providing access to facilities or experience;

■ helping you use software.

2 Who might be able to provide these and similar forms of help?
Start by brainstorming all the possibilities.

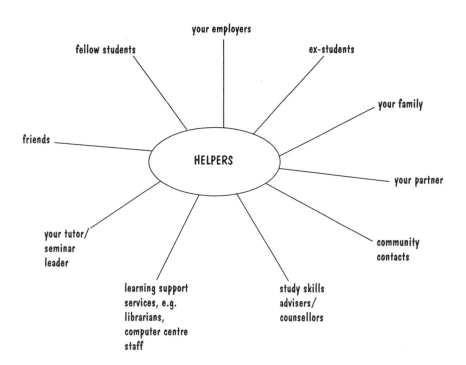

All these are possible sources of help. You probably thought of others. Note that the particular 'label' used to describe a person will vary depending on the context. In some cases – nursing and social work training for example – you are encouraged to choose a **mentor** to help you study.

Different people can give different kinds of help, depending on their experience and position. You would, for example, probably go to an academic member of staff to get a detailed up-to-date reading list; to a librarian for help in finding the books.

3 Complete the table below, using for now the following options: a friend, another student, tutor, librarian, employer. (You will be able to include other sources of help in your own action plan for this unit.) If there are several possible sources of help, list them in order of priority.

(continued opposite)

Type of help	Person likely to provide
Discuss possible time management targets	
Give encouragement	
Give information on the programme	
Explain what assignments require	
Discuss approaches to assignments	
Collect resources for assignments	
Give access to certain equipment or experience	

Type of help	Person likely to provide
Discuss possible time management targets	Friend; another student; employer(?)
Give encouragement	Friend; another student; employer
Give information on the programme	Tutor; librarian(?); another student(?)
Explain what assignments require	Tutor; another student; librarian(?)
Discuss approaches to assignments	Tutor; another student; librarian(?)
Collect resources for assignments	Librarian; employer; another student(?)
Give access to certain equipment or experience	Employer; tutor

Who will help will, of course, depends on the nature of the course and the context. You might have different responses from mine, and there is no right answer. But I hope the activity shows:

- that people can help you manage your time;

- that in most cases you can choose from a range of possible people;

- that different people can give different kinds of help.

People within your own institution

Some key people will be working within the services provided by your own institution, such as librarians, technicians, counsellors. These services are covered in the section on *Making the most of the facilities your institution provides* in Unit 10.

But one group is particularly important: your fellow students. Unit 9 looks at one rather negative aspect of this: the interruptions you might experience from others. But of course your colleagues can also be the source of great informal support as well. Unit 1 suggests you could work on this book together with other students. You also have a lot to gain from helping one another on your course. Sharing books and discussing assignments are obvious examples.

You may be required to work together formally, too, as a part of your course. Group projects, for which you are assessed, present particular time management challenges.

(There's an example in Unit 4.) Group members need to support each other, for example by:

■ attending, and preparing for, meetings;

■ completing their share of the work on time;

■ sharing the 'chores', such as getting resources together.

In group projects you will realise that, while you may be able to control your own time, you cannot necessarily control the time of others. Your time efficiency will be affected by the efficiency of the group as a whole.

You may thus have to invest time and effort in getting the group to work productively, using the assertiveness skills described in Unit 9 if necessary!

Action plan

You can now pull together the work you have carried out on this unit so far, by completing the action plan. Draw up a table like the one below.

The first stage of your action plan is to decide:

● what type of help you personally would like;

● who you think could provide it.

Complete your table.

Type of help	Person likely to provide it

Approaching people for help

You now need to approach the people you have decided can help you. They may be individuals, or part of a service (such as a library). Approaching them can be broken into the following steps:

1   preparation;

2   asking for the help;

3   agreeing a plan;

4   carrying out the plan;

5   reviewing the plan.

Step 1: Preparation

I shall concentrate on the first stage, which is also the key to the others: preparation.

The amount and type of preparation you need will depend on the situation. For example, asking a friend for help is less formal than asking your employer. Some people give help as part of their job; others do so voluntarily, as a favour. Whoever you ask, you will need to be precise in saying what it is you want.

Example

General area: giving encouragement.

You have drawn up a plan to improve your time management. You think your main difficulty will be keeping to the plan. You choose a fellow student with whom you share a flat. You decide that the specific things you want your friend to do are:

- to comment on your plan, especially whether it is realistic;

- to encourage you to stick to it by asking each week about progress.

This will take only a few minutes and you think your friend will be quite interested anyway. Also, you know your friend has a difficult assignment coming up, one you can help with.

The Other Steps

Such preparation takes a little time but it makes the remaining steps much easier. These are set out below.

> **Asking for the help**: make sure the time and place are right for this. You may need to make an appointment.

> **Agreeing the plan**: including the duration of the help and when you will review progress.

> **Carrying out the plan**: supported as appropriate by your helper.

> **Reviewing progress**: either on your own, or with your helper. Evidence of success will often be enough reward for the person who helped you.

My parents have been to stay and have 'taken over' my chores and left me in peace in the study for a day at a time.

The kids have been good. They think it's funny Mum studying, but they do help with shopping and washing up.

Action plan (Part 1)

Now turn back to your own situation and prepare to ask for help.

Use the questions to help you take any necessary notes.

- What help do I want?

- What do I want the helper to do? Over what period of time?

- What benefits will the helper get (if they are volunteers)?

- When and where will I approach them to plan the help?

- How and when will I review progress?

We contract with each other, for example we'll all work for two hours in the library and then go for a drink together.

Instead of each person in our house preparing their own meal, we decided to share the task. So only one of us shops and cooks each day. This frees up one to two hours, which the other five people can use for study.

Other sources of help

Another obvious source of help in planning your time is a diary. Diaries vary greatly in the facilities they offer. At their simplest they give you the space to record your fixed appointments. This is the function most people immediately think of.

The organiser

More recently 'organisers' have been designed to support a wider range of time-management activities. Sometimes they are accompanied by instructions on how to use a bewildering array of expensive stationery. Organisers are a combination of time planner, diary and database – with space for information such as names, addresses, telephone numbers, birthdays and expenses.

Organisers can be used to support the various activities discussed in this book, such as:

■ scheduling tasks for more than one project (Unit 3);

■ drawing up a resource plan over a defined period (Unit 5);

■ prioritising and scheduling tasks (Unit 6);

■ planning over different periods, such as a year, a month, a week, a day (Unit 7).

Various specially designed forms are usually produced for these purposes: day planners, weekly planners, project planners and so on. The loose-leaf format means you can insert or remove pages whenever you like and easily reorganise the contents.

It's worth visiting stationers to look at organiser systems for yourself. Popular newsagents and department stores usually keep a range of such products, including some at cheaper prices. You might find a use for a total system. Or you may prefer to buy an empty ring binder and insert just a few of the forms that suit you own needs. For example, I find the pull-out 'year planners' very helpful. You can also buy blank and lined paper, for making your own notes, and dividers, that allow you to separate the notes relating to your various projects.

Think about the best size for your circumstances. Sizes range from A4 through to small organisers that genuinely fit a pocket. The more portable ones mean you can consult your papers easily at odd moments, such as while waiting for a train, and add to them. You could, for example, keep notes on your forthcoming assignment topics. When necessary, you can transfer these to a larger ring binder or notebook.

You may decide to make up your own forms. This saves money. It also means you can devise a system to suit your own particular needs. The paperwork is basically simple, as shown in Unit 7.

Such stationery enables you to translate your goals into specific targets, with dates and times attached. Your organiser becomes a working document. As such it won't be neat; it will be full of tentative plans made and remade. So it helps to use an easily erasable pencil.

Checklist

Ask yourself the following questions about organisers:

- What sections will I need?
- Do I need a full system or only certain pages?
- What size do I need?
- Will I design my own pages?
- How much can I afford to spend?

Electronic Organisers

The various hand-held electronic organisers carry out similar functions to the paper-based versions. These products cost between £50 and £500 (1994 prices). The bottom end of the range allows you to store basic data such as names, addresses and telephone numbers; as you spend more you get more sophisticated features, some of which would certainly help you carry out the planning tasks described in this book. Electronic organisers tend to be expensive, so it is rare to see students with them. Do you need one? The checklist of points below should help you decide.

Checklist

Do I:

- need to carry around a lot of interconnected information in a compact form?
- frequently change this information?
- need frequently to gain access to this information?
- need to store confidential information?
- find it hard to read my handwriting?
- need alarm calls?
- have the money?

If most answers are YES then you might find an electronic organiser a useful investment. The more powerful organisers will not only store and display information, they will also sort it for you, for example into date or alphabetical order. You usually need to weed out data frequently, every month for example, so you will not be able to store large quantities of information.

If you decide to buy an electronic organiser, use the following checklist to help you weigh up alternatives. It is not an exhaustive list, but it should get you started.

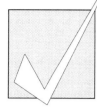

Checklist

- How much does it cost?
- What does it weigh?
- How long do the batteries last? What do replacement batteries cost?
- Can the organiser be plugged into the mains?
- Is the memory protected if the power runs out?
- Does it have a QWERTY keyboard?
- Is the display clear?
- Is a calculator included?
- How much memory is there? (128k is ideal.)
- Are there short cuts to putting in data?
- Is it easy to use?
- Are help screens included?
- What other devices can be connected to the organiser (for example personal computer, printer)?
- Will it show one week's diary on a screen?
- Does it have a project management capability?

Courses

Courses are another source of help with managing your time. Educational institutions sometimes put these on, covering time management on its own or as part of a broader approach to learning skills.

Action plan (Part 2)

Draw up a table like the one below and record any actions you wish to take in relation to organisers (paper or electronic) and courses.

Action: what you have decided to do.

Dates: for starting and finishing the action.

Review: for comments on your progress and on any further actions you will carry out.

Action	Dates	Review

UNIT 13 REVIEWING YOUR PROGRESS

What this unit is about

This unit will help you:

→ explain the importance of **feedback**;

→ review your progress towards using time more effectively;

→ plan your next steps.

Time: approximately 20 minutes to work through the unit; a further 10 minutes planning.

Resources: file paper.

Using feedback

Good performers spend time reviewing their skills. This applies to sport, to the theatre – and to study. As Unit 1 pointed out, improving your skill requires constant practice (including trying new things out) and reflection. Reflection then leads on to further practice, as experience helps you to identify the next things you want to try. As a student you should take every opportunity to review your progress, using feedback from others whenever possible.

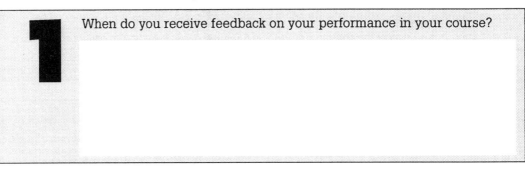

1 When do you receive feedback on your performance in your course?

You usually get this from tutors, for example on an assignment or exam. You probably also get feedback from other students, for example during a group project or presentation.

A review model

This unit sets out a simple model of purposeful behaviour. You can apply this, using the accompanying checklists, to improving your time management skills. You can also apply it to other areas of your life, where you wish to perform more effectively, such as sport or hobbies.

There is a further reason for spending time systematically reviewing your progress: assessment. New-style programmes require evidence of such review. The criteria for **GNVQ** Level 3, for example, require students to be assessed on 'the way they retrospectively review. . . the activities they undertake; the decisions taken in the course of that work; examination of alternative courses of action which they might have adopted; and examination of the implications of particular courses of action' (from *Implementing BTEC GNVQs: A Guide for Centres*, BTEC, June 1993).

Thus you may actually be assessed on your ability to be constructively self-critical.

The review cycle

As you know, action planning is built into every unit in this book. The steps are:

■   set your targets;

■   plan how you will reach them;

■   carry out the plan;

■   review your progress;

■   set new targets.

This is better set out as a cycle, as below.

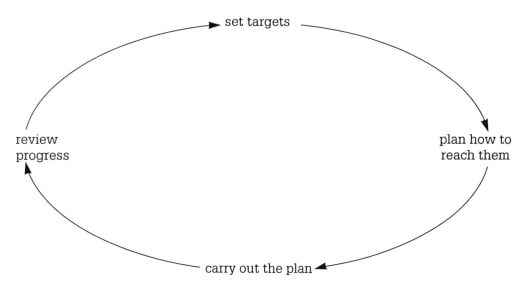

Notes on each stage follow.

Set targets

The book suggests you set general goals for improving your time management skills. Then you turn these into specific targets. You should first check that your goals are the right ones. The Pareto Principle (see Unit 11) should help you with this.

When you turn goals into targets you should make sure they meet the criteria set out below.

The criterian are easy to memorise: Targets should be SMART:

Specific: so you know exactly what you're trying to achieve.

Measurable: so you can recognise success.

Action-orientated: the action you will take is clearly set out in the verb, e.g. 'write', 'list', 'file'.

Realistic: so you can achieve it and build your confidence.

Time-bound: you set a time by which you will have achieved the target.

Read the following example. Is it SMART?

At the end of each weekday I shall spend approximately 10 minutes planning the next day's activities, and enter them in my diary, with an approximate time allowance for each.

Yes, I think this is SMART. The target is:

Specific: activities, with approximate times, for each weekday.

Measurable: the student can measure progress by looking at the diary entries.

Action-orientated: the action is clearly shown by the verb phrase 'enter in my diary'.

Realistic: the task will take only a few minutes each day, and should become a habit.

Time-bound: the job is done at the end of each weekday.

Unit 6 has further work on target setting.

Plan how to reach the targets

The action plans in each unit have been designed to help you plan how to reach your targets. Planning includes deciding:

■ what resources you will need (for example materials, people, time);

■ how you will collect them;

■ start and finish dates.

Your plan should include key points, at which you can measure your progress. The following example shows points at which progress could be measured.

Example

● All resources collected by now.

● Notes for essay completed.

● Essay outline finished.

● First draft word processed.

Carry out the plan

You put the plan into operation. As you do this, you should monitor it constantly: is the plan working out?

Don't hesitate to change your plans if you have good reason to do so. You may, for example, find that some stages take more time and others less. Or more pressing and unexpected priorities may need your attention. If you monitor your progress, for example by noting against your plan what you actually achieved, you get valuable data to help you in the future. You can, for example, leave more time for some tasks, less time for others, create more slack to respond to emergencies, and so on.

Example

The example shows a student's analysis of how long tasks actually took, compared to the time estimated.

Task	Estimated time	Actual time
Interviews	3 hrs	5 hrs 30 mins
Write up notes	6 hrs	3 hrs 40 mins
Draft	2 hrs 30 mins	1 hr 45 mins

This will help the student adjust time allocation in the future.

Review progress

At this stage you review what you did at all the earlier stages. The questions in the checklist should help.

Checklist

Set targets

- Have I reached my targets?
- Did I achieve them in the time and with the resources planned?
- If I did not succeed, why? Was I too ambitious? Did unforeseen circumstances get in the way?
- Did I achieve any additional targets?

The plan

- Did I choose the best route to achieve my targets?
- Did I change my plan along the way? Why?

Carrying out the plan

- Which parts of the plan went well?
- Which parts of the plan went badly?
- What problems did I meet? Did I overcome them? How?

Review progress

- What did I learn about myself and how I work best?
- What would I do differently next time?

Set new targets

- What new targets do you want to set?
- Are they SMART?

> I'd never thought about the need to review. I just got on with the work. Now I look critically not only at the results but also at how I got there.

Conclusion

You should practise the above sequence for all your planning, until it becomes second nature. You will then become increasingly skilled at taking the initiative, not only in managing your time as a student but in your career and life more generally.

This is the end of the book. It is a good time to wish you luck with your future time management. We can all continue to improve: no one becomes the perfect time manager! The final action plan will help you review your progress since starting this book.

Action plan

Review your action plans for any units you have tackled in this book. Use the questions in the above checklist as a guide. Conclude by setting yourself new targets.

Return to the diagnostic questions about time management at the end of Unit 1. Look at the answers you gave when you first encountered these questions. Are your answers different now? Are your priorities different from when you first answered?

GLOSSARY

Assignment: a piece of work that you submit for assessment. An assignment may take many forms. It may be written or word processed; it may be an object, such as a wall you have built or a meal you have cooked.

Brainstorm: to brainstorm is to think up a lot of different ideas, as creatively and quickly as possible.

CD-ROM: CD-ROM stands for compact disk read-only memory. It is a means of storing data. The user gains access to the data via a computer.

Competence: effectiveness in carrying out tasks, particularly of a practical or vocational kind.

Course: the programme of study for which you are enrolled, for example a certificate or diploma programme or a **National Vocational Qualification.**

Criteria (assessment/performance criteria): standards or measures used to assess your work, for example on **assignments**.

Database: a collection of information. The term usually describes data stored on a computer. Access to this is usually 'on line' (via a computer network) or 'off line', for example on a **CD-ROM**.

Feedback: information you get on your performance, for example a tutor's comments on an **assignment**.

General/National Vocational Qualification (GNVQ, NVQ): national qualifications awarded for the demonstration of competence, either directly in the work environment (NVQ) or, more generally, in preparation for work (GNVQ). In Scotland, NVQs are known as SNVQs.

Icon: a symbol used on a computer screen (for example a wastepaper basket or file).

Mentor: a person who helps you in a variety of ways, for example by discussing your progress. You agree with the mentor the help that he or she will provide.

Menu: a list of options available on a computer screen.

Module: component part of a **course**. The term 'unit' can also be used. See Unit 2.

National Vocational Qualification (NVQ): see **General/National Vocational Qualification.**

Objective: what you seek to achieve in your learning. See **outcome**.

Outcome: the end result of a particular study activity, for example a report, a meal. 'Learning outcome' is used to describe what you can show for your learning. Outcomes are closely linked to assessment: your outcomes are assessed to determine how effective your learning has been.

Portfolio: a collection of documents and other evidence, usually submitted for assessment. The term is used particularly to describe a collection of evidence organised by a candidate for an **NVQ** or **GNVQ**.

Term: a defined period of time during which you study (as opposed to the 'vacation'). Some institutions now call this period a 'semester'.

Window: an opening on a computer screen, to show particular information, such as **menus** or help screens.

APPENDIX
2

FURTHER READING

This is a list of books you may find helpful for further work. You are not expected to buy or borrow all or indeed any of these books. They are simply suggested as optional extras, if you wish to work further on particular learning skills.

General books on studying

The following books cover a wide range of learning skills.

Freeman, Richard and Meed, John *How To Study Effectively*, Collins Educational and the National Extension College, 1993

Northedge, Andrew *The Good Study Guide*, Open University Press, 1990

Assessment

Henderson, Penny *How to Succeed in Exams and Assessments*, Collins Educational and the National Extension College, 1993

Writing

Lewis, Roger *How to Write Essays*, Collins Educational and the National Extension College, 1993

Inglis, John and Lewis, Roger *How to Write Reports*, Collins Educational and the National Extension College, 1993

Stress management

Livingston Booth, Audrey *Stressmanship*, Severn House, 1985

Assertiveness

Back, Ken and Back, Kate *Assertiveness at Work*, McGraw Hill, 1982